Hearty Food
for Hungry Folks

WESTERN
COOKING

Hearty Food For Hungry Folks

WESTERN COOKING

by Lois McBride

David McKay Company, Inc.
New York

Library of Congress Cataloging in Publication Data

McBride, Lois.
Western cooking.

Includes index.
1.   Cookery, American—The West.   I.   Title.
TX715.M116
641.5'978   76-13635
ISBN 0-679-50635-7 pbk.
ISBN 0-679-50598-9

Manufactured in the United States of America
Designed by The Etheredges

For Tom, and Mark, and Lee —
who make the difference
for me

CONTENTS

INTRODUCTION

In my family, with its roots more than a hundred years deep in the West, cooking was never a dry, cookbook procedure. Recipes were never "written down," but were in the minds and memories of the cooks—and cooking was fun.

My grandmother and her four sisters would gather in the kitchen and their quick Scotch-Irish wit flew faster than their fingers, with many a pause in the cooking while they bent double or leaned against the wall, helpless with laughter. While they cooked they told stories or reminisced or regaled each other with penetrating, hilarious comments on people and places and life, and laughed until their tears streamed. Great-aunt Elizabeth never liked to cook and made no bones about it, but Joan and Isabelle and Lottie and Virginia cooked with the same flourish and style that greased their wit.

Their brothers were cowboys in the high loveliness of Idaho, tough, witty men who loved a life their children could scarcely wait to leave. They cooked out of chuck wagons and sheep wagons and over sagebrush fires, with Uncle Mark providing a "mixed grill" of sage hen, grouse, quail, and trout—all out of season and therefore out of the law.

My grandfather—a French-Indian with black eyes, a hooked nose, and a smell of horses and Bull Durham—I remember for coffee out of an enameled pot he never washed and for bacon fried golden and crisp and then slapped between buttered sourdough biscuits that were a good three inches high. His sister was a lady of elegance and graciousness, and was without a doubt, the finest cook I ever knew.

We ate in the kitchen of a ranch called "The Hat" where wild hay grew sweet and high, and Antelope Creek ran forever, with enough trout to catch to entertain a little outdoor girl. We ate in cozy sheep wagons, perched near the airtight stove, with our knees bumping and the wind a frenzy beyond those curved canvas walls; and we ate outside on the prairie—all of us except Aunt Elizabeth, who acidly commented that she "never could understand people who went inside to the toilet and outside to eat."

I grew up thinking that food was defined as much by people feeling good about each other, and life itself, as it was by its taste.

The West Coast port cities—Seattle and Vancouver and incomparable San Francisco—taught me the gusto of Italian coast cooking and the excitement of Chinatown cafés. My husband courted me with brook trout fried by a tiny fire in the Charnack Basin of Nevada; and we have shared bread and cheese and scalding tea in fiercely free wildernesses in Idaho, Montana, and Canada. There have been memorable moments made of steamed clams on the thunderous North Pacific coast, and sandwiches made of watercress and sardines in the Sierra Nevadas. I remember pots of lentil soup on long tables in Basque restaurants in Nevada; tacos and enchiladas and guacamole and sopaipillas in New Mexico; tea stirred with a peppermint stick in Wyoming. I've craved smoked salmon, which I first discovered in Oregon; and I've made pies of rhubarb and wild strawberries in an abandoned cabin buried deep in the Salmon River wilderness of Idaho, where we watched bighorn sheep from our window.

Being happy while eating frontier-style is by no means limited to the West. Cook IDAHO BEANS in a Chicago kitchenette; buy the ingredients for

LOST RIVER POTATOES in Miami; serve SOUP-STEW to friends you love in Newark. You can make sourdough bread in a subdivision kitchen or a townhouse apartment as well as in a log cabin. The simplicity and hospitality of frontier cooking travel well, as the wagon trains proved a century ago.

Frontier cooking was originated by men—trappers, traders, and scouts coming to the West before they were sure it was there; and the cowboys and cattlemen who followed them, carrying scanty food supplies in their bedrolls. They cooked over campfires on the prairies and in the mountains, making do with a cast-iron skillet, a coffee pot, and a cup.

The cooking of the frontier had to stay simple, even for the women who came to live on lonely homesteads and raise a pioneer generation. They had limited supplies, limited equipment and facilities, and limited time. To cook frontier style was to cook creatively, right from the beginning.

Frontier cooking wears time as well as it wears distance. A hundred years ago it was scarcity that limited the supplies in a housewife's pantry; today it's the high cost of living that limits them. Today's women have different obligations and have-to-do's to crowd their hours than did the yesterday ladies, but time is still limited—and time-saving recipes and cooking ideas are just as precious now as they were then. The only thing that remains exactly the same is the heartiness of the appetites that must be satisfied.

Breaking bread with laughter, together on some piece of earth, is an act of love. This cookbook is a collection of food I've enjoyed, remembered, lived on, and loved by. Stories are an inseparable part of the recipes. A recipe's roots—why and how it came to be, where we savored a certain dish, the laughter that accompanied it, a few tender moments and a few bittersweet—are somehow stirred into the ingredients. Therefore, this is more than just another cookbook. It is also a love story.

Instead of salmon-soufflé-on-a-Limoges-plate or Salad-Caesar-in-a-crystal-bowl, we give you beans and friends; coffee and trails; peaks and valleys and the wild, free land we love.

LOIS MCBRIDE
The Crow's Nest
September, 1975

Chapter 1

HEARTY SOUPS AND SOUPS AS A MAIN COURSE

Soups are nourishing, filling, inexpensive, and a warm welcome on a cold winter day. Make a stout soup and serve it with hot rolls and cold milk for lunch, or add a salad and a simple dessert to make a friendly dinner. Make a thin soup vigorous by adding tiny dumplings on top. Extend a soup with rice or macaroni or even broken pieces of spaghetti. Combine two soups to make a unique third. Experiment with seasonings—add a dash of curry to plain potato soup or a sprinkle of cloves to tomato.

Soups are a stimulant to the creative urge. Invent your own soup or create variations of any soup recipe. It's hard to ruin a pot of soup.

In the old days, soup in a blue enamel canning kettle or a black cast-iron pot simmered gently on the back of a wood range. It was ladled into generous bowls whenever anyone came in feeling "a little bit gaunt."

SUPPER SOUP
(SERVES SIX)

A pot of soup can be the main course of a dinner. This splendid soup, served to us in the breathtaking beauty of Jackson Hole, Wyoming, was accompanied by fruit salad and hot biscuits with currant jelly.

6   *medium carrots, scraped and chopped*
4   *medium potatoes, peeled and chopped*
1   *medium onion, peeled and chopped*
2   *stalks celery, chopped*
1   *quart tomato juice*
1   *pint water*
2   *teaspoons salt*
½   *teaspoon pepper*
¼   *teaspoon marjoram*
¼   *teaspoon basil*
½   *pound hamburger*
1   *teaspoon salt*
¼   *teaspoon pepper*
     pinch sage
1   *egg, beaten slightly*
½   *cup uncooked oatmeal*
1   *tablespoon milk*
1   *tablespoon flour*

Put first 10 ingredients in a large kettle and simmer until vegetables are tender—about 30 minutes. Add more water, if needed, for plenty of broth. Combine remaining ingredients, mixing well, and shape into small balls, a tablespoon at a time. Drop into soup, cover, and simmer until done—about 25 minutes.

SOUP-STEW

(THIS WILL SERVE SIX AMPLY, BUT IT CAN MULTIPLY
LIKE LOAVES AND FISHES AND FEED MORE
IF YOU THIN IT WITH WATER.)

This stewlike soup is a full dinner with the addition of crusty bread or rolls for sopping in the broth. It is simplicity itself to make—flavorful, nutritious, and inexpensive. I think it is a loving welcome on cold days, a comforting thing for recuperating virus victims, a cozy Sunday supper, and a treat when it is warmed up for my own breakfast. Make lots—it keeps well and gets better as it ages. Don't be afraid to add water to thin it down and stretch it out. Just readjust seasonings to taste.

1	pound hamburger
1	quart water
1	#303 can tomatoes, mashed
1	onion, peeled and chopped
3	potatoes, pared and cut in bite-sized chunks
3	stalks celery, sliced
3	small carrots, scraped and thickly sliced
½	teaspoon pepper
¼	teaspoon oregano
¼	teaspoon garlic powder
¼	teaspoon basil
	salt to taste
1	cup (or 1 buffet can) whole kernel corn
1	cup (or 1 buffet can) string beans
½	cup uncooked rice or pearl barley

In a large kettle break up uncooked hamburger and add water, tomatoes, onions, celery, potatoes, carrots, and seasonings. Cover and simmer gently 1 hour. Add corn, beans, and rice or barley. Simmer 45 minutes, or longer if you have more time. Add hot water with the last 3 ingredients if more broth is wanted, and re-season if necessary.

MEXICAN SOUP

(SERVES FOUR)

There is a silent, bleak beauty to the desert, particularly the deserts of the American West, where a dim purple line of mountains is a reminder on the horizon. The land seems ancient—rocks are worn to the bone and the mountains' ribs are showing. In the spring, for a short space of time, desert land is carpeted with vast sweeps of red, blue, yellow, purple, and pink as miles upon miles of wildflowers bloom.

For the pioneers lumbering west in wagons, the deserts were barriers as formidable as the looming mountains; and scattered across the desert are stark testimonials to the pioneers' struggle—wagon wheels, sun-twisted trunks and dressers abandoned to lighten heavy loads, rusted iron, and lonely graves of those who died of hunger, thirst, and despair.

The desert is a secretive world, hiding springs in willowed gullies and abandoned mines on the slopes of mountains. There was such a mine on such a mountain, where my husband, Tom, and I feasted on boiled coffee, MEXICAN SOUP, and cold biscuits; watched twilight come; and remembered the struggle of people we had never known.

1	*small onion, peeled and chopped*
2	*tablespoons butter or margarine*
1	*tablespoon flour*
½	*teaspoon pepper*
1	*teaspoon salt*
1	*tablespoon sugar*
1	*teaspoon chili powder*
1	*#303 can whole kernel corn, undrained*
1	*#303 can tomatoes, mashed, with juices*
2	*cups water*

Cook onion in margarine for about 5 minutes, stirring constantly. Add flour and blend well. Add remaining ingredients, stirring to blend as you add, and simmer gently 30 minutes.

TOMATO SOUP
(SERVES SIX)

My husband's career as a wildlife photographer—and our own inclinations —take us often into wild, roadless country via foot travel or horseback.

Some trips are enchanted from beginning to end, and nothing goes wrong; some have ups and downs, with problems we solve as they happen; and some are so plagued with mishaps that we wish we had never started.

One dismal trip even started poorly on a September day in Idaho, with rain and wind and troublesome horses. We traveled nearly twenty miles, untangling stubborn packhorses and fighting wet rope and canvas, and reached our camp just at nightfall with a real storm threatening to break at any moment. We piled supplies, still packed, under a piece of canvas; fed horses and turned them out; covered saddles and equipment; found a meager supply of wood; and built a weak fire. I fished around in pack boxes in the dark for *something* for dinner, and my first two reaches produced a large can of tomatoes, a packet of instant milk, and a tub of margarine. Then and there I invented tomato soup—regardless of what the Campbell Soup people may think.

1   *28 ounce can (# 2½) tomatoes*
1   *quart milk or 2 cups milk and 2 cups water*
    salt and pepper to taste
    butter or margarine

Buy a very large can of the cheapest tomatoes you can find. Drain the juice into a large saucepan. Mash the tomatoes with your potato masher (or your fingers) and add to the juice. Add milk and season to taste with salt and pepper. Simmer very gently 10 minutes. Serve with a dab of butter in each bowl.

I learned later that this soup stretches further and tastes great with the addition of a cup or two of cooked macaroni or rice. Even without the stretcher you will have 1½ quarts of soup for a little over half the price of commercially prepared soup. If you like thicker soup, thicken the juice with flour or cornstarch before you add the rest of the ingredients.

POTATO SOUP

(SERVES FOUR)

The Pacific Coast is a study in contrasts from the sunny, hospitable beaches of the south to the moody sea in the north, where the surf rushes and crashes endlessly on black rock cliffs.

We have wandered the beaches from San Francisco northward, wading tide pools and climbing to sea caves, watching at night with lanterns for the grunion runs that come in a silver tide, searching for treasures in driftwood, and feasting on POTATO SOUP when the sea catch was slim, with our feet propped up over a sunset.

3	*large potatoes, cooked, peeled and diced*
1	*quart milk*
1	*onion, peeled, chopped, and sautéed in butter until transparent*
2	*tablespoons butter or margarine*
1	*tablespoon flour*
1½	*teaspoon salt*
¼	*teaspoon pepper*
	dash cayenne
2	*tablespoons butter or margarine*
2	*tablespoons chopped parsley or green onion tops*

Scald milk with sautéed onion. Add to cooked potatoes. Melt 2 tablespoons butter, add flour and seasonings, and blend well. Stir into hot soup. Boil 1 minute. Top with remaining butter and parsley. (This is even better if you sauté 1 stalk celery, chopped, with the onion, or add 3 slices bacon, fried crisp and crumbled; and is downright important if you add fresh clams or small oysters and simmer until their edges curl—about 5 minutes.)

Pepper

CARROT SOUP
(SERVES FOUR)

Missionaries from the Mormon Church nearly 150 years ago went on expeditions all over the world, fired with religious conviction and spreading their new gospel. Many converts returned with them to the United States to walk a thousand miles pulling handcarts to Utah and their "promised land." Many of the pioneering converts were Scots, and they brought to the West an honest accent and a taste for tea and a solid, honest soup.

When I make CARROT SOUP, I sometimes do as my Scotch ancestors often did and add a leftover pork or lamb chop to make the broth richer.

1	*small potato, peeled and finely diced*
1	*cup thinly sliced, scraped carrots*
1	*small onion, peeled and thinly sliced*
½	*teaspoon sugar*
½	*teaspoon pepper*
1	*teaspoon salt*
2	*cups milk*
1½	*cups water*
¼	*cup butter or margarine*

Cook vegetables and seasonings in water to barely cover until vegetables are tender—about 20 minutes. Drain, saving water. Measure water and add an additional quantity to make 1½ cups. Add to vegetables. Add milk and season to taste. Reheat about 5 minutes or until hot enough, and add butter as you serve.

HAM AND POTATO SOUP
(SERVES FOUR)

HAM AND POTATO SOUP is another hearty "Made in Scotland" import, a perfect solution to the uniquely Western expression "I'm so hungry I could eat the north end of a southbound cow!"

2	*cups water*
2½	*cups diced peeled potatoes*
1	*cup thinly sliced celery*
½	*cup peeled, chopped onion*
1	*quart milk*
1	*to 2 cups diced leftover ham*
3	*tablespoons butter or margarine*
	salt and pepper to taste

In a kettle gently simmer potatoes, celery, and onion in water to cover until just tender—about 20 minutes. Drain well. Return to kettle with remaining ingredients. Simmer gently 10 minutes, stirring often, and serve piping hot.

MARK'S SPLIT PEA SOUP
(SERVES SIX)

When our dark-eyed son was small, this was his favorite soup. On frigid winter days he would come in, snowy-clothed and rosy, and toast himself before the fire—warming fingers and stomach at the same time with a mug of this soup. While he toasted, I dried his clothes so he could go back out and repeat the process. Sometimes we would join him in the lovely dusk, making angels in the snow and listening to our own laughter.

2   *cups split peas, soaked overnight in 2 quarts water*
1   *meaty ham bone or 2 ham hocks*
½   *teaspoon pepper*
1   *cup finely chopped celery*
1   *large carrot, scraped and shredded*
1   *onion, peeled and finely chopped*
2   *cups beef bouillon*
1   *cup milk*
2   *frankfurters or German sausage, sliced thinly*
     salt to taste

Bring soaked peas to a boil, adding water if necessary. Reduce heat, add ham bone and pepper. Cover and simmer 1 hour. Add celery, carrot, and onion. Simmer 1 hour longer. Remove ham bone. Pull off meat and shred it finely. Return meat shreds to soup and add remaining ingredients. Simmer 20 minutes.

CORN SOUP
(SMALL SERVINGS FOR FOUR)

When I was about fifteen, romantic and in love with beauty and the poetry of Edna St. Vincent Millay, my family lived for a time on the lovely, wooded California coast a few miles north of San Francisco.

On one foggy autumn afternoon, I climbed a high hill near our house where there were no houses or people to distract a young girl with a highly developed sense of drama. From the top of the hill, through shifting veils of fog and rain, I saw the opening lines of Millay's poem "Renascence." As I looked out, turning slowly on my stormy height, there were the "three long mountains and a wood" and, as I turned further, there were "three islands in a bay."

I went home cold and ecstatic, wet and bedraggled with streaming hair, and luxuriated in a yellow kitchen with a bowl of CORN SOUP. I remember that my mother sprinkled a few grains of cinnamon on top of the soup.

1   #303 *can cream-style corn*
1   *cup water*
1   *cup milk*
¼   *cup finely minced onion*
     salt and pepper to taste

Combine all ingredients in a saucepan. Stir well. Simmer gently 10 miuntes, stirring frequently.

QUICK SOUP
(SERVES SIX)

More than once we have come in, cold and hungry, from a snowy day outside and I have started this pot of soup, leaving it to take care of itself while I did other things. After it is well launched, all it needs is an occasional brisk stir as you walk past the stove to break the ground meat into small pieces as it cooks.

2   *quarts water*
1   *pound hamburger*
1   *onion, peeled and chopped*
½   *cup uncooked rice*
1   *cup chopped celery*
3   *cups peeled, diced potatoes*
1   #303 *can tomatoes, mashed*
1   *teaspoon salt*
½   *teaspoon pepper*
½   *teaspoon chili powder*
¼   *teaspoon marjoram*

Put all ingredients in a large kettle and bring quickly to a boil. Reduce heat, cover, and simmer 45 minutes. Add a cup of any leftover cooked vegetables you might have on hand, and additional water if necessary. Re-season to taste and heat through again.

CREAM OF VEGETABLE SOUP
(SERVES FOUR)

Leftover vegetables accumulate in all refrigerators. A dab of this and a dab of that sit in little dishes, doing nothing, until somebody's twitching sense of thrift is dulled and they are finally thrown out. In the unapologetic, thrifty attitude of the West, they often have a happier ending in this soup.

2   *large potatoes, peeled, quartered and boiled*
1½   *to 2 cups any kind or combination of leftover cooked vegetables*
1   *small onion, peeled and thinly sliced*
3   *cups milk*
        salt and pepper to taste

Drain cooked potatoes and mash. Add vegetables and mash roughly to blend into potatoes. Stir in milk. Add hot water, if needed, to make a medium-thick soup. Simmer 10 minutes, stirring frequently, and season to taste. Nice to serve with a lump of butter in the bowls.

KRAUT SOUP
(SERVES SIX TO EIGHT)

Since I'm not passionately fond of sauerkraut, I avoided this soup for a long time before I finally got curious enough to try it. After the first taste, I was sorry that I had waited so long and missed all the good bowls of excellent soup at which my stubbornness had turned up its nose.

This soup is served often at a pioneer-flavored luncheon restaurant in Helena, Montana, where a pretty girl named Mary makes it. She let me muddle around for weeks, tasting and trying to figure out the ingredients, before she confided that the thing that makes the difference is NOT draining the sauerkraut.

1   *large ham bone*
3   *quarts water*
2   *onions, peeled and chopped*
3   *stalks celery, sliced*
1   *bay leaf*
    salt to taste
1   *teaspoon pepper*
1   *#303 can sauerkraut, undrained*
1   *#303 can tomatoes, mashed*
1   *cup shredded cabbage*

Place ham bone and water in large kettle and simmer, covered, for 1½ hours. Add onions, celery, and seasonings, and simmer 15 minutes. Mash tomatoes and add with undrained sauerkraut. Simmer at least 30 minutes, an hour if possible. Add cabbage and simmer until cabbage is tender— about 20 minutes.

Serve with pumpernickel bread and bowls of salad made of crisp greens and chilled vegetables.

CROW'S NEST SOUP
(SERVES SIX HUNGRY PEOPLE)

We live now in the mountains of western Montana. Our home is a big, old, log house named *The Crow's Nest* because Crow Indians once erected a large tipi there. It perches on a pine-wooded mountainside near the head of a lovely canyon, at the end of a dirt road that winds along a creek. Outside, there are Volkswagen-sized granite boulders scattered among the pines— quiet, sun-warmed spots for reading and dreaming. Inside, the old log walls have, through the years, turned the color of dark honey.

On the walls are my husband's photographs of bighorn sheep and high, far places. Books are there, and music, and the smell of wood smoke, and friends we love. When night quiets the mountains, the only lights we can see are our own. We sit on the floor with wooden bowls of CROW'S NEST SALAD and brown pottery bowls of CROW'S NEST SOUP and thick wedges of tangy bread.

4   or 5 beef marrow bones, or meaty neck bones, or oxtails
1   #303 can tomatoes, mashed
4   stalks celery, sliced diagonally, with a few of the tops, diced
2   medium onions, peeled and coarsely chopped
3   large potatoes, well scrubbed but not peeled, cut into bite-sized
    chunks
½   teaspoon coarsely ground pepper
¼   teaspoon garlic powder
    salt to taste

Put bones and tomatoes in kettle with water to 1 inch over top of bones. Simmer 3 hours. Add remaining ingredients and simmer 1 hour longer, adding hot water, if needed, for lots of broth.

Chapter 2

FRONTIER WAYS TO STRETCH MEAT (BEEF, VEAL, LAMB)

There were few dinners in the old Western days that did not revolve around meat. Most of the old cowboys—line riders for the big ranch spreads like Miller and Lux or the King Ranch or the Scissorbill outfit, or those who rode their own lonely ways—hunched over their campfires and fried steaks done to the near-cremation stage in cast-iron skillets. The women, keeping an even heat in their wood-fed ranges, did a better job.

These recipes represent the various flavors of people who blended to make the West.

OLD-STYLE COMPANY ROAST

(SERVES FOUR TO SIX)

I think this way of preparing roast was invented when a frontier lady dallied too long gossiping over the fence and let her wood range go out. It is a good method for today, conserving fuel as it does.

The secret is to keep the oven door closed so the heat that continues to cook the roast stays in the oven to do its job instead of escaping into the kitchen. The roast will be done on the outside, shading from medium to rare as you slice toward the center.

1   *4- to 5-pound rib or rump beef roast*
1½   *teaspoons salt*
¼   *teaspoon pepper*
¼   *teaspoon garlic powder*

Let roast stand at room temperature for at least 1 hour before cooking. Blend seasonings and rub on meat. Place, fat side up, in greased roasting pan. Preheat oven to 400° F. Reduce heat to 375° F. and roast meat for 1 hour. Turn off heat. Do not open oven door until 30 minutes before dinner, allowing roast to stand in closed oven for 1 to 1½ hours. Reheat at 375° F. for 30 minutes before serving.

POT ROAST

(SERVES SIX)

There are expressions and phrases native to each region of the United States, and the West has its own colorful sayings. Americans as a group are ever ready to change their language and have readily adopted such Western words as "maverick" and "dude."

In the West, the statement "It's getting a little bit Western out there" means that the weather is building up to a near-blizzard. "He's a little bit mortal" translates "He's drunk."

A "hay-wire rig" means a patched-together thing that might come apart any minute, while "all rigged up" is something that is fixed-up and ready to go—be it horse, fishing rod, or person. "Duded up," on the other hand, means all dressed up in your finest "duds"—and *that* means clothing.

"Dark as the inside of a cow" is very dark indeed—as dark as "a stack of black cats." A container filled to the top is "plum full," and something that tastes very good is "larrapin'." To "wallop your dodger" means to push a bite of bread or biscuit around your plate to soak up the last traces of gravy or meat juices, and "fixin's" are either the ingredients that go into a dish or the side dishes that accompany meat.

It is odd that there are few expressions for excellence. Part of the lack is due to a feeling that it is bad form to brag openly. If a cowboy has an excellent horse, for instance, and someone said, "That's a great, marvelous, magnificent, tremendous horse you have there!" the cowboy would be apt to reply, "Yep." The closest thing to a superlative expression I can think of is "damn fine."

When my grandfather got up from my grandmother's cooking—pot roast with black gravy, whipped potatoes, stewed tomatoes, Waldorf salad, two kinds of pie, and coffee—he would nod in her direction and say, "Damn fine meal, woman."

This is her pot roast, and it is a damn fine one.

1   *4- to 5-pound blade, chuck or arm pot roast, at least 2-inches thick*
    salt and pepper to taste
3   *to 4 tablespoons cornstarch*

Brown roast in hot fat in a heavy dutch oven. When browned on both sides, pour on 1 cup boiling water. Cover and cook at a very slow simmer about 3 hours, turning often and adding hot water, a cup at a time, just as the previously added water cooks away and the meat almost starts to burn. The roast is done when it is fork-tender. Remove from the dutch oven and keep hot.

The dutch oven will have fat and a gummy black substance on the bottom. Pour off excess fat, leaving about ¼ cup in the dutch oven. Add 2½ to 3 cups hot water, stirring madly to scrape up all that lovely blackness. Thicken with cornstarch and season to taste with salt and pepper. Bring to a boil, reduce heat promptly and simmer 5 minutes.

My grandmother often added strong hot coffee instead of water when the pot roast was reaching the done stage.

I must admit that this method results in a very well-done roast—but it is good, and this is the only way to achieve that savory black gravy.

GYPSY-DAY POT ROAST

On the bird feeder outside the window are all at once a male hairy woodpecker, a chickadee, two Oregon juncos and a red-breasted nuthatch, while a Canada jay is cheerfully stealing from the dog food pan on the kitchen patio. Last Sunday a beautiful brown bear was sitting on his round behind just 16 feet from the back door, and in the evening there was a bull moose—black and shiny and big—in the shallows at the pond up the gulch. I saw a cross fox cross the road, and one summer dusk a mother coyote was playing with two of her pups in the old lane by the cabin. With so much going on, how can I stay indoors? Write your name in the dust on the bookcase and wash a cup if you need one. I'm going out, and we'll eat GYPSY-DAY POT ROAST tonight:

Put a 4- to 5-pound round-bone or 7-bone pot roast in an oiled roasting pan and season with salt, pepper, garlic powder, and a sprinkle of Liquid Smoke. Cover pan and put in a cold oven—at eight in the morning. Turn oven to 150° F. Forget about the whole thing and spend the day outdoors. As six or seven in the evening—whenever you gather for dinner—serve slices of the roast, done to tender perfection, with hot applesauce, steamed fresh broccoli, and slices of brown bread. (If the roast is going to cook less than 10 hours, set the oven temperature initially for 200° F.)

STUFFED FLANK STEAK

(SERVES FOUR)

Flank steak is a tough cut of beef and, therefore, is much less expensive than more tender cuts. Stuffed, tied, and baked, then sliced in 1½-inch pinwheels and served with its own sauce over it, it is fine enough for company dinner when you want a special menu.

1   *flank steak*
1   *recipe—about 2½ cups—bread dressing (see recipe in Chapter 7, "Potatoes and Other Fillers.")*
2   *cups hot water*

Spread stuffing over steak, roll it up like a jelly roll, and tie it securely in several places. Roll gently in flour and brown in hot fat in a baking pan. Pour water over roast. Cover and bake at 350° F. for 1½ hours.

When the meat is tender, remove to a hot platter. Thicken the pan juices with 1 tablespoon flour. Slice steak (do not remove strings until steak slices have been placed on each plate) and dress each slice with a tablespoon of the sauce.

BAR-B-Q FLANK STEAK
(SERVES FOUR)

1	*flank steak*
1½	*cups hot water*
1	*teaspoon prepared mustard or ½ teaspoon dry mustard*
1	*8-oz. can tomato sauce*
¼	*teaspoon tabasco sauce*
1	*teaspoon lemon juice*
1	*tablespoon Worcestershire sauce*
1	*medium onion, peeled and minced finely*
1	*clove garlic, minced finely*
1	*bay leaf*
1	*stalk celery, minced finely*
¼	*teaspoon thyme*
¼	*teaspoon pepper*

Combine last 12 ingredients and heat briefly in a saucepan, stirring to blend. Put steak in a flat baking dish and lightly score in a crisscross pattern with a sharp knife.

Pour about ⅓ cup sauce over steak. Cover and bake at 325° F. for 1½ hours, basting steak with sauce about every 20 minutes.

WESTERN STEW

(SERVES FOUR)

A book in frontier cookery wouldn't be complete without a recipe for
WESTERN STEW. You won't find a ranch, a chuck wagon, or a high camp in
which sooner or later you won't be served stew. (I even know of one down-
at-the-heels hunting camp in which the camp cook would, on the first day in
camp, make an enormous canning kettle full to the brim with stew—
which he served breakfast, lunch, and dinner for days on end.)

2   *pounds stew meat, cut into 1½-inch chunks*
4   *tablespoons flour*
1½   *teaspoons salt*
¼   *teaspoon pepper*
1   *15-oz. can tomato sauce or 2 cups tomato juice*
2   *large onions, peeled and chopped*
3   *potatoes, pared, quartered, and cut into bite-sized pieces*
2   *stalks celery, thickly sliced*
2   *medium carrots, scraped and sliced*

Dredge meat in flour and brown in hot fat in a heavy kettle. Season with
salt and pepper. (Sometimes I add a shake of garlic powder and a pinch of
oregano.) Add remaining ingredients, cover, and simmer slowly 1½ to
2 hours.

If you have on hand some leftover vegetables, such as corn, string
beans, peas, or zucchini, by all means add them to the stew about 15
minutes before you call it done.

WESTERN BOILED DINNER

As I understand it, a New England Boiled Dinner is a tradition based on
corned beef. In the Northwest, we most frequently use short ribs, or what
is called around here "boiling beef."

short ribs, 2 for each person, depending on appetites. One each will
be sufficient for children or those with less aggressive appetites.
small whole pared potatoes—figure on 2 per person, again depending
on appetite. You can use the same quantity of halved larger
potatoes.
small whole peeled onions—1 per person, with an extra in the pot
for good measure.
small whole scraped carrots—2 per person.
1 small head cabbage, quartered and cored.

Put ribs in a large kettle, cover with cold water, and bring slowly to a boil. Reduce heat, cover, and simmer slowly until almost tender, 1½ to 2 hours. Keep water level over beef and add hot water as needed. When meat is nearly tender, add potatoes, onions, and carrots. Season to taste with salt and pepper—we like ours a little more peppery than usual. Cook 20 minutes, or until carrots are nearly done. Add cabbage and cook 20 minutes longer. Cabbage should be barely tender, not soggy. Arrange meat on a large platter with the vegetables around it. Serve the "pot likker" (or "pot liquor," to be proper) in a separate bowl or save for delicious broth.

Coleslaw or fruit salad and hot rolls are made to order to accompany this savory, casual dinner.

IDAHO SUKIYAKI
(SERVES FOUR)

I had a relative in an old Idaho cowtown who was forever taking a trip somewhere, a craggy-faced cowboy who dressed in Levis and boots, to whom the world must have held a quality of wonder. He always traveled by bus, and once went to San Francisco to visit relatives. They took him on a tour of San Francisco's Chinatown for dinner in Chinese and Japanese restaurants, and on treks up and down the streets of high excitement. When he got back to Idaho, his only comment was: "Them fellers can *cook.*"

That was too much for the family cooks, who promptly invented Idaho versions of Chinatown cuisine. This is one of their efforts. I can't help contemplating with some amusement the expression on the face of the one grocer in their town when they waltzed in and grandly asked for canned bamboo shoots.

    4   *tablespoons cooking oil*
    4   *cups sliced celery*
    2   *onions, peeled and thinly sliced*
    1   *cup chopped green onions*
    1   *4-oz. can mushrooms, drained*
    1   *8½-oz. can bamboo shoots, drained*
    2   *firm tomatoes, sliced*
    1   *10-oz. can consommé, undiluted*
    ½   *cup soy sauce*
    3   *tablespoons sugar*
    1   *quart whole washed spinach leaves*
    1   *pound round steak, sliced thinly*

Put oil in a large skillet and add celery, onions, green onions, mushrooms, bamboo shoots, and tomatoes. Cook gently 10 minutes. Add consommé, soy sauce, and sugar, stirring. Add spinach and steak. Cook about 15 minutes more, stirring frequently. Serve with rice.

IDAHO CHOP SUEY
(SERVES FOUR)

It wasn't sufficient, of course, to rest on Sukiyaki laurels. The ladies went on to master their version of chop suey—and did a good job of it.

    1½   *to 2 pounds round steak, cut into cubes*
    1   *medium bunch celery, cut into ½-inch slices*
    2   *onions, peeled and sliced*
    ½   *bottle soy sauce—about ½ cup*

Brown steak cubes in butter or oil. Add celery and onions. Cover with water. Stir in soy sauce. Simmer 45 minutes.

Serve over rice and top with crisp Chinese noodles.

BARBECUE STEAK
(SERVES SIX TO EIGHT)

A Western rodeo is a colorful show—and, by the way, you can get away with pronouncing it row-DAY-oh, Spanish style, in California, but you'd better say it ROW-dee-oh in Idaho and Montana.

The West goes first class with a rodeo. The cowboys are invariably virile, lean-hipped, and sun-bronzed, wearing tight Levis and snap button shirts. Rodeo clowns are fearless and funny, the bulls ferocious, the bucking horses pitch and buck and sunfish in the air, and some hapless cowboy usually takes a spectacular spill. The spectators get their vicarious thrills and wear Western hats and boots to make themselves part of the scene. There are smells of sweat, leather, dust, horses, and a trace of fear; and there are sounds to remember made of the soft slap and creak of leather and hoarse voices saying, "easy . . . whoa, whoa there . . . ho, now . . . easy," and a pulsating roar from the grandstand.

Many Western rodeos are held in conjunction with the county fair, and often local clubs or businesses present a Western-style barbecue to top off the whole production. The rodeo barbecues traditionally serve green salad, corn on the cob, and barbecued beef. Big barbecues cook a whole beef—or two; middle-sized affairs barbecue roasts; and small rodeo barbecues take steaks to a succulent finish.

1	*cup ketchup*
½	*cup water*
¼	*cup vinegar*
¼	*cup chopped green pepper*
¼	*cup peeled and chopped onion*
1½	*tablespoons Worcestershire sauce*
1	*tablespoon mustard*
4	*tablespoons brown sugar*
½	*teaspoon salt*
¼	*teaspoon pepper*
¼	*teaspoon garlic powder*
¼	*teaspoon rosemary*
4	*pounds round or chuck steak, cut 1-inch thick*

Combine all ingredients except steak in a saucepan, bring to a boil, reduce heat, and simmer slowly 5 minutes.

Pound steak to tenderize and cut into serving portions. Put in a large roasting pan and pour barbecue sauce over the steak. Cover and bake in a 325° F. oven for 2 hours, or until meat is fork-tender.

OXTAILS

"Colorado" is one of my favorite words, along with "windowsill" and "serenity." I like to say it because it fills my mouth—not heavily, like mashed potatoes, but lightly, like whipped cream.

It is also a marvelous place to be, with its dramatic beauty. In the splendid mountains there are enough honest ghost towns to satisfy the most hopelessly vagabond heart—towns that were born of the search for gold, lived a shorter or longer span of adventure and excitement, then slipped away into shadows.

There was Boreas Pass, bleak and lonely in the wind, built to service the little narrow-gauged railway that once freighted silver ore; Beartown, left to silence after the throbbing days when ore poured from mines like the Gold Bug and the Good Hope; Carson City, sitting right on top of the Continental Divide, once a boomtown, now derelict and alone; Mayflower, weather-beaten and restless in its sleep; Lake City; Capitol City; Henson; Holy Cross City, with a mine called Hunky Dory and one of the most beautiful views in the West; enchanted Leavick; Horseshoe; the mining town called Buckskin Joe that was the home of a dance-hall girl named Silverheels; Tin Cup, wild town of violence and dark.

It was in Denver that I first tasted oxtails, and had something else to remember about Colorado.

Oxtails are about what they sound like. They are the tails of beef, cut into segments along the joints. Obviously, they are mostly bone, but the bits of meat are flavorful. Cooked long and slowly to make the meat tender, they are truly delicious. Flavorful, easy to prepare, and inexpensive—those are good recommendations for any recipe.

You will need at least 3 oxtail joints for each person—or more, depending on the size of the joints. I get a dozen for our family of four.

COLORADO OXTAILS
(SERVES FOUR)

½   *cup cooking oil*
12   *oxtails*
1   *cup flour*
      salt
      pepper
⅛   *teaspoon garlic powder*
      sprinkle of ground sage

Heat oil in a large, heavy Dutch oven. Dredge the oxtails in flour and brown well on all sides in the hot fat. Season liberally with salt, pepper, garlic powder, and a light touch of sage. Pour on hot water to cover the browned oxtails. Bring the water just to the boiling point, reduce heat, cover tightly, and simmer slowly for a long time—at least 4 hours. Peek under the lid every now and then, and add boiling water as needed to keep the water level even with the top of the oxtails. When the oxtails are nearly tender—after about 3½ hours—stop adding hot water. Re-season, and let the water simmer down to about halfway up the meat.

Serve the oxtails on a platter, with the self-made gravy over hot, buttered noodles.

RANCH HASH
(SERVES FOUR TO SIX)

Earth must be the loveliest of planets, spinning like a glowing jewel through space, harboring wilderness in which to walk.

If I were an antennaed, green visitor from space, looking at maps of the universe to plot a pioneer journey, I'd set my destination for the North American continent of the planet Earth. I would zero in on the Northwest, and make a gentle landing in Idaho. I do believe, strange pioneer I, that I would walk or waddle up to the nearest log cabin in the nearest mountain valley and say, "May I have some RANCH HASH, please?"

about 4 cups cooked, ground leftover meat or boiled stew meat
3   *large potatoes, peeled*
3   *large onions, peeled*
½   *cup bacon drippings*
1   *teaspoon salt*
¼   *teaspoon pepper*
¼   *teaspoon garlic powder*
     sprinkle of ground sage

Put leftover roast or boiled stew meat through coarse blade of food grinder until you have about 4 cups of ground meat. Place in a large, flat baking dish. Grind potatoes and onions, and stir into ground meat. Add remaining ingredients. Pour boiling water over all, stirring as you add, until mixture is quite "soupy." Bake in a 350° F. oven until mixture has "set" and is starting to get crispy around the edges—about 1½ hours.

When I was a little girl, there was a traditional menu served around RANCH HASH. In spite of the potatoes *in* the hash, we always had baked potatoes *with* the hash and a simple salad made of lettuce chopped into a bowl and topped with a layer of thinly sliced radishes and then chopped tomato. My mother would thin mayonnaise with heavy ranch cream, season it with salt, pepper, and a quick dash of cayenne, and gently pour the dressing evenly over the salad.

I always hoped—and still do—that hash would be left over in a sufficient quantity to reheat in a skillet in the morning to go under breakfast poached eggs.

PASTIES
(SERVES SIX)

During the gold rush days of California, from the 1850's into the 1890's, miners from the Cornwall country of England came to the gold fields to work their way into a new life. Cousin Jacks, they were called, hearty, honest men who sang and laughed and added their flavor to the melting pot of the West.

They carried to the mines lard buckets, filled with hearty food for their lunches—hot tea, roasted apples, and little meat pies called PASTIES. These are good either hot or cold, and are a filling lunch.

4　　cups flour
　　　salt and pepper
1½　cups shortening
½　　cup cold water
¼　　cup butter or margarine
2　　pounds lean round steak, cubed
3　　potatoes, pared and cubed
2　　onions, peeled and chopped
3　　carrots, scraped and chopped in small pieces
　　　pinch garlic powder

Sift flour with 2 teaspoons salt; cut in shortening. Work with hands until flour is the consistency of cornmeal. Add water and mix. Pastry will be moist. Roll dough into six 10-inch circles.

Melt butter and add remaining ingredients, with salt and pepper to taste. Spread meat mixture over half of each circle. Moisten the edge of one half with water and fold it over meat. Seal the edges together by pressing with fork tines. Brush each pasty with milk. Cut small slits in each top so steam can escape. Bake on cookie sheets at 425° F. for 10 minutes. Reduce heat to 325° F. and bake 1 hour.

OCTOBER POT ROAST

Autumn must be glorious everyplace. In the West it's a golden time. The aspen turn leaves to a shimmer of bright gold, and in the conifer forests, the tamarack—the black pine that lose their needles during the winter— turn a darker shade of gold with an undertone of red. The air is tangy, and there is a compelling excitement in the atmosphere. It's impossible to stay indoors. That's when I cook a lot of pot roasts—this one in particular, loaded with nutrition and painlessly quick to prepare.

¼ cup cooking oil or melted fat
1   4- or 5-pound round bone or blade pot roast
4   large potatoes, well scrubbed but not pared, cut in quarters
3   onions, peeled and halved
4   stalks celery, cut in 4- or 5-inch lengths
4   carrots, scraped and cut in halves
3   parsnips, scraped and cut in halves

Preheat oven to 400° F. Put cooking oil or melted fat in large roasting
pan. Put pot roast in pan, cover, and place in oven. Reduce heat to 325° F.
Turn every hour. Bake for 3½ hours. Place vegetables under meat. Season
liberally with salt and pepper. Add 1 cup very hot water. Cover roasting
pan and continue cooking 45 minutes. Turn roast one last time, and bake
20 minutes longer.

MEAT IS MORE THAN BEEF

Italians settled in New York before they found San Francisco, and so did
the Irish. The Chinese were shipped from Oriental ports to the West Coast
and migrated east. The Basque came to the West straight from Europe, and
stayed there.

The Basque are native to the Pyrenees, the storied mountains separating
Spain from France, but these people are neither French nor Spanish. They
are not a cultural blend but a people all their own. Their language bears
no resemblance to any other language. It is impossibly difficult—dreadfully
complex to speak and a strange thing to see in print, but gentle and liquid
to the ears. Nevada and southern Idaho ring with the proud old family
names of Yrigoyen and Eschiverria which represent the Basque.

They are sheep or vineyard men. In California they grow wine grapes,
and in Nevada sheepmen long ago learned that Basque sheepherders are
second to none.

The sheepherders lead a lonely life, lost in an empty land of thousands
of acres of sagebrush and rock, living in lurching sheep wagons that become
their only real home. They have only their dogs and the sheep to speak to
as they follow the sparse grass from desert floor to mountain and back again.
The echo of the wind is forever in their ears, and their eyes grow dim with
thousands of sunrises.

My great-grandfather employed three Basque—Fidel, Spidel, and

Martine. Fidel worked for great-grandpa before my mother was born, and
when I was a grown woman I met him on the streets of an Idaho cowtown
—frail and bent and well over ninety years old. He didn't know me but he
remembered my great-grandfather, and I gently led him down the generations until he found me in his memory.

Fine Basque cooks are hard to beat. They do delicious things I don't
know how to do with goat meat and cook a lamb roast in a paste of garlic
and butter. The Basque restaurants in Nevada, in places like Minden,
Garnerville, and Carson City, serve dinners family-style at long tables—
and you'd better be on time because everyone sits to dinner at the same
time. There are big bowls of soup, based either on a rich meat or chicken
broth or a superb lentil soup, and then bowls of lettuce in a vinegary dressing. The rest of the dishes arrive in quick succession: bowls of peas or string
beans, mashed potatoes and gravy, platters of spaghetti with a gravy, and
veal cooked in a thick, highly seasoned sauce. Chicken is fried to a heavy
crust and then simmered in wine and herbs. There are round loaves of bread,
each scratched with a cross before it is cut, and glasses of dark wine.

BASQUE VEAL

(VEAL IS COSTLY NOW, BUT A LITTLE GOES A LONG WAY AND THERE IS
MINIMAL WASTE. THIS RECIPE SERVES SIX PEOPLE WITH ONLY BAKED
POTATOES AND A SIMPLE GREEN SALAD TO ACCOMPANY IT,
AND FRUIT FOR DESSERT.)

1	*2-pound veal steak, ½-inch thick, boned*
2	*tablespoons flour*
1	*teaspoon salt*
1	*cup minced, peeled onion*
3	*tablespoons melted fat or cooking oil*
1	*teaspoon prepared mustard*
1	*bouillon cube*
1	*cup boiling water*
1	*cup dairy sour cream*
½	*cup white wine*
¼	*teaspoon basil*
¼	*teaspoon garlic powder*
¼	*teaspoon savory leaf*
1½	*tablespoons cold water*

Flatten steak with a mallet to ¼-inch thickness. Cut into six pieces. Sprinkle
with 1 tablespoon flour mixed with ½ teaspoon salt.

Sauté onion in 2 tablespoons oil in a heavy skillet until tender. Remove
from skillet. Add 1 tablespoon oil to skillet and sauté veal pieces until they
are golden on both sides. Add onions, mustard, and bouillon cube dissolved
in 1 cup boiling water. Cover and simmer over low heat 45 minutes.

Remove veal to hot platter. Add sour cream, wine, and remaining
seasonings to pan drippings. Heat thoroughly but do not boil; stir in mixture made of remaining salt, remaining flour, and cold water. Cook,
stirring, until thickened. Pour over veal.

BASQUE LAMB CHOPS

(AS IT IS WITH VEAL, LAMB IS EXPENSIVE. THIS RECIPE CALLS FOR LAMB
SHOULDER CHOPS—A MUCH LESS EXPENSIVE CUT—AND WILL SERVE
FOUR TO EIGHT PEOPLE DEPENDING ON THE AMOUNT OF
SIDE DISHES YOU SERVE WITH IT.)

8	*shoulder lamb chops*
	salt and pepper
	flour
2	*tablespoons butter or margarine*
2	*tablespoons cooking oil*
1	*clove garlic, thinly sliced*
1	*small peeled onion, thinly sliced*
1	*4-oz. can mushrooms*
1	*cup chicken bouillon*
¼	*cup tomato juice*
	hearty pinch nutmeg
¼	*cup grated Parmesan cheese*

Season flour with salt and pepper. Dredge the chops in the seasoned flour. Melt butter in a heavy skillet and add oil. Sauté garlic and onion. Remove from skillet. Brown chops on both sides. Return garlic and onion to chops and add mushrooms, bouillon, tomato juice, and nutmeg. Cover and cook over low heat 30 minutes, gently stirring occasionally. Add more liquid if necessary. Sprinkle with cheese and let stand 10 minutes before serving.

BROILED LAMB CHOPS BASQUE STYLE

(USE LESS EXPENSIVE SHOULDER CHOPS IN THIS RECIPE, AND COUNT ON
IT TO SERVE FOUR TO EIGHT PEOPLE. FOR EIGHT, JUST
INCREASE THE QUANTITIES OF SIDE DISHES.)

8   *shoulder lamb chops, 1-inch thick*
½   *cup cooking or olive oil*
1   *tablespoon rosemary*
½   *teaspoon garlic powder*
1   *teaspoon thyme*

Mix oil and seasonings, and pour over chops in a flat pan. Cover and refrigerate for several hours, turning chops occasionally in the marinade.

Broil 5 inches from the heat. Cook until done to the stage you like best—that will be about 10 minutes on each side for medium—basting now and then with the marinade.

MAKE PEACE WITH HAMBURGER

Hamburger doesn't have any ham in it. It's beef. It is also inevitable in your diet—unless you have a lot of money and don't mind spending it—so you might as well accept it gracefully. You can do a great many different things with hamburger to vary its taste and appearance, but you must have a satisfactory grade of hamburger to start with.

Some markets grind meat with a lot of fat and increase its weight with quantities of water. The result boils away in your skillet, leaving you with a little meat and a whole lot of grease. Avoid that unhappy situation by not selecting hamburger that is a sickly pink in color. Good hamburger is a vigorous red.

Meatloaf is one of the most common hamburger recipes. It is also one that can drift very easily into a rut, so try different meatloaf recipes in order to dodge boredom.

MEATLOAF WITH FORETHOUGHT
(SERVES FOUR TO SIX)

2   *pounds hamburger*
1   *cup uncooked oatmeal*
1   *beaten egg*
1   *medium onion, peeled and chopped*
2   *teaspoons salt*
¼   *teaspoon pepper*
¼   *teaspoon poultry seasoning*
¾   *cup milk*

Mix ingredients together thoroughly. Form into a loaf in a heavy skillet and bake at 350° F. for 1 hour. When done, gently remove meatloaf from skillet to a serving plate and let it sit for a few minutes before slicing. Put the skillet on top of the stove and adjust heat to medium. Add 2 cups water to the drippings, stir well, and bring to a boil. In a jar with a tightly fitting lid, put 3 tablespoons flour and ½ cup water. Shake like mad until mixture is smooth, then pour slowly into the skillet, stirring constantly, until gravy has thickened. Reduce heat and simmer 5 minutes. Season with salt, pepper, and a whiff of marjoram.

Don't serve gravy with the meatloaf! Have baked potatoes with the meatloaf, and use the gravy later in the week over hot meatloaf sandwiches, noodles, or rice.

GLAZED MEATLOAF
(SERVES SIX)

The Pahsimeroi Valley of Idaho is high and wild and empty, stretching from one line of purple mountains to another, with one end tipping toward the Salmon River and the other end tipping into the sky. Antelope run like quicksilver and race the wind, and eagles trace effortless circles in the air. It is a magic place, filled with a silence that is heavy with life you sense rather than see. In little draws (what Westerners often call gentle, sloping canyons between hills—usually those with a small creek running down them) and valleys tucked away on the edges of the mountains are a few long-abandoned log homestead cabins, left derelict with a tracery of fence and a boxed-in spring, where men with visions beyond their means left their dreams.

We once camped on the edge of the Pahsimeroi, in a sagebrush flat at the foot of Double-Springs Pass, and tried to find a phantom band of big-horn sheep to photograph. We spent an enchanted day, drifting through the vastness with the eagles and the wind, and at dusk met a solitary mountain lion which moved with such easy grace that there was no question that we were in the presence of royalty.

We followed the old wagon road back to our little trailer camp, and ate GLAZED MEATLOAF to celebrate the occasion as it was the finest thing we had.

1½	pounds hamburger
¾	cup uncooked oatmeal
¾	cup milk
1	medium onion, peeled and chopped
½	teaspoon dry mustard
1	egg, slightly beaten
1½	teaspoons salt
¼	teaspoon pepper
½	cup jelly, any kind
1	teaspoon dry mustard
1	tablespoon brown sugar

Combine first 8 ingredients and mix well. Shape into a loaf and bake at 350° F. for 45 minutes. Beat jelly with mustard and brown sugar, and spread over top of meatloaf. Return to oven and bake 15 minutes longer.

Serve with baked potatoes and buttered carrots.

ITALIAN MEATLOAF
(SERVES FOUR TO SIX)

Many Italian pioneers settled in the great interior valleys of California, where they planted magnificent vineyards and made great wines or created tidy truck gardens for an ever-hungry market. They didn't forget how to make cheese, and you will use some of it in this recipe. If your local market doesn't carry ricotta cheese, you can substitute small curd cottage cheese if you press the moisture out of it.

1½   pounds hamburger
1   cup soft bread crumbs
2   eggs
½   cup grated Parmesan cheese
½   onion, peeled and either grated or minced finely
¼   cup milk
½   teaspoon basil
2   teaspoons salt
¼   teaspoon pepper
½   pound ricotta cheese

Mix meat with crumbs, 1 egg, Parmesan cheese, onion, milk, ¼ teaspoon basil, 1½ teaspoons salt, and pepper. Pat half of the mixture into a 9"×5"×3" loaf pan. Mix ricotta with 1 beaten egg, ¼ teaspoon basil and ½ teaspoon salt. Spread over meat. Pat out remaining meat and press on top of cheese. Bake in a 350° F. oven for 1 hour. The cheese melts and some of it oozes out during the baking. Spoon it back over the slices of meatloaf.

CRUNCHY GRANOLA MEATLOAF
(SERVES SIX TO EIGHT)

The mountains of Montana have marvelous names. They sprinkle through the legends of the West—the Absarokas, named after the word the Crow Indians used to identify themselves; the Beartooths; Tobacco Roots; the Crazy Mountains; the Bridgers. They rise to the sky from the plains: Big Belts, the Snowy Mountains, Beaverhead, Bitterroots, Missions, Gallatins,

Flatheads, the Salish, the Cabinets, the Kootenais. I love to say their names and remember them, seeing in my mind's eye how they soar above the prairies—wild and jagged and unfettered.

I love even more to walk in them—and we do, often, gypsying through golden days with backpacks. One of the trail foods we carry is granola, and I've learned to use that nutritious mixture in at-home foods as well. One of the most successful inventions is this hearty meatloaf.

2	*pounds hamburger*
1/4	*cup milk*
1 1/2	*cups granola*
1	*egg, slightly beaten*
1	*small peeled onion, diced*
2	*teaspoons salt*
1/4	*teaspoon pepper*
1/3	*cup chili sauce or ketchup*

Combine ingredients and mix well. Pack into a loaf pan and bake at 350° F. for 1 hour.

Serve with a vegetable plate and stewed fruit, such as rhubarb.

KITCHEN SINK MEATLOAF
(SERVES SIX TO EIGHT)

When my grandmother had to produce in a hurry a dinner she hadn't expected to cook, she simply started moving, with implicit faith that something would come to mind. She would start with hamburger, rummage through refrigerator and cupboards, and then announce grandly over the entirely acceptable results: "There's everything in that but the kitchen sink!"

1½   *pounds hamburger*
½   *of an 8-oz. can tomato sauce*
1   *small onion, peeled and chopped*
2   *cups uncooked oatmeal*
1½   *teaspoons salt*
½   *teaspoon pepper*
¼   *teaspoon oregano*
½   *cup grated cheese*

ONE *of the following:*

2   *cups bread dressing;* OR
1   *#303 can drained whole kernel corn;* OR
1   *#303 can drained peas and 2 cups mashed potatoes;* OR
1½   *cups cooked rice blended with ½ of an 8-oz. can tomato sauce*
     and ¾ cup water

Mix hamburger with ½ can tomato sauce, onion, oatmeal, salt, pepper, and oregano. Pat mixture into the bottom and sides of an ovenproof casserole. Fill the center with EITHER bread dressing OR corn OR a layer of peas topped with a layer of mashed potato OR rice blended with tomato sauce and water. Cover with lid or foil, and bake 30 minutes in a 350° F. oven. Uncover, top with cheese, increase oven temperature to 375° F., and bake 15 minutes longer.

Serve with vegetable fritters and a fruit salad.

MEATBALL GAMES

Meatballs are still hamburger and are suspiciously like meatloaf, but they are much more fun to make and have an appeal to anyone who ever enjoyed making mud-pies. They are helpful in avoiding boredom with hamburger.

MEAT PUFFS
(SERVES SIX)

1½ *pounds hamburger*
1 *cup scraped, shredded carrots*
2 *cups peeled shredded potato*
½ *cup peeled, finely chopped onion*
1 *egg, beaten*
1 *cup fine bread crumbs*
1 *teaspoon salt*
¼ *teaspoon pepper*
 pinch marjoram
2 *tablespoons flour*
1 *cup milk*

Combine ingredients, cover, and refrigerate 1 hour. Fill well-greased muffin tins with the mixture and bake at 350° F. for 30 minutes.
 Serve with a vegetable, stewed fruit, and dessert.

SAVORY MEATBALLS
(SERVES SIX TO EIGHT)

2 *pounds hamburger*
1 *cup uncooked oatmeal*
1 *egg, beaten*
1 *medium onion, peeled and chopped*
2 *teaspoons salt*
¼ *teaspoon pepper*
½ *cup milk*
1 *8-oz. can tomato sauce*
1 *cup brown sugar*
⅓ *cup vinegar*
¼ *cup cooking or salad oil*
⅓ *teaspoon basil*
½ *teaspoon rosemary*
¼ *teaspoon garlic powder*

Combine first 7 ingredients and shape into balls the size of an egg. Brown lightly in a greased skillet and remove to an ovenproof casserole dish. Combine remaining ingredients and stir to blend. Pour over meatballs and bake, covered, at 350° F. for 25 minutes. Uncover and bake 20 minutes longer.

Serve with baked potatoes and a green salad.

MEATBALLS AND BIG WHITE
(SERVES FOUR TO SIX)

I had a relative who was a somewhat independent character. A bachelor all his life, he was for some time pursued by a lady of advancing years and dubious charms, who also happened to be the worst cook in town. Although he successfully avoided her for months, she finally backed him into a corner and he couldn't find a way out of having dinner at her house.

He arrived home at a remarkably early hour and his sister, wild with curiosity to find out what happened, casually asked him what he had for dinner. He replied by describing a dish of boiled potatoes and gluey milk gravy as "'taters and big white."

Milk gravy or white sauce has remained "big white" in our family to this day. Unlike that of the smitten lady of old Arch's experience, this dish with white sauce is *good*.

1	*pound hamburger*
3	*small carrots, scraped and grated*
½	*cup celery, finely chopped*
1	*pound potatoes, peeled and grated*
½	*cup uncooked oatmeal*
1	*egg, beaten*
1½	*teaspoons salt*
½	*teaspoon pepper*
¼	*teaspoon garlic powder*
¼	*teaspoon marjoram*
2	*cups medium white sauce*

Combine all ingredients except white sauce and shape into balls the size of an egg. Brown in hot fat in a skillet. Put in a baking dish and pour white sauce over. Cover and bake at 350° F. for 45 minutes.

Serve with marinated, chilled vegetables, buttered noodles, and a tart dessert.

WEST TO THE ORIENT

The Orient, with all its exotic glamour of the different and the far away, is really just over the horizon of the West. These two recipes, which make something uncommon out of common hamburger, indicate the Oriental influences that threaded through every state on the Pacific side of the Rockies.

They were there, those beautiful people of the Orient, in every Western mining town. People like me who love to poke around ghost towns and old cabin ruins sometimes find treasures left behind by Chinese miners—a rusted old wok, the slope-sided, handleless frying pan from China; a ginger jar; or a fat-bodied, brown ceramic bottle that once held the Chinese wine called *ng-ka-py*.

ORIENTAL MEATBALLS
(SERVES FOUR)

1½	*pounds hamburger*
2	*eggs*
3	*tablespoons flour*
	salt and pepper
¾	*cup cooking oil*
1½	*cups chicken bouillon*
3	*green peppers, coarsely chopped*
6	*slices pineapple, diced*
1	*medium onion, peeled and chopped*
2	*tablespoons cornstarch*
2	*tablespoons soy sauce*
¾	*cup vinegar*
¾	*cup pineapple juice*
¾	*cup sugar*
½	*teaspoon salt*

Shape meat into 18 balls. Make a batter out of the eggs, flour, salt, and pepper. Dip meatballs in batter and fry gently in oil until browned. Remove and keep hot. Pour all but 1 tablespoon oil out of skillet. Add ½ cup bouillon, green pepper, pineapple, and onion. Cover and cook over low heat 10 minutes. Mix remaining ingredients and add. Cook, stirring, until mixture thickens. Add meatballs and simmer 15 minutes.

Serve with rice and spinach.

FAR OUT MEATBALLS
(SERVES FOUR)

1½	pounds hamburger
½	cup granola
¼	cup milk
1	egg, beaten
2	tablespoons horseradish
1	teaspoon salt
¾	cup orange marmalade
1	clove garlic, mashed
3	tablespoons soy sauce
¼	cup peanut butter

Combine all ingredients and form into balls the size of a walnut. Brown lightly in hot oil in a skillet. Reduce heat, cover, and simmer gently 20 minutes, stirring occasionally.

Serve with buttered rice and cooked, frozen peas.

CASSEROLES

My personal list of great inventions would have to include casserole recipes along with safety pins and toilet tissue. A casserole combines meat; a vegetable, a "rib-sticker," or both; and a tasty sauce—all in one economical, time-saving, nutritious package.

WAGON WHEEL CASSEROLE
(SERVES SIX)

1   *pound hamburger*
1   *cup ripe olives*
2   *stalks celery, sliced*
1   *large green pepper, thinly sliced*
¾   *cup peeled, chopped onion*
1   *cup uncooked rice*
2   *tablespoons cooking oil*
1   *#2½ can tomatoes, mashed*
2   *teaspoons salt*
1   *tablespoon chili powder*
½   *teaspoon pepper*
4   *or 5 dashes tabasco sauce*
2   *slices quick-melt cheese*
    (Monterey Jack or American)

Brown beef lightly in a large skillet. Transfer to a 2-quart ovenproof casserole. Combine olives, celery, green pepper, onion, and rice in skillet with cooking oil, and sauté until rice is lightly browned. Add tomatoes with liquid and remaining ingredients except cheese. Bring to a boil. Pour over meat in casserole, cover, and bake at 350° F. for 1 hour. Uncover and arrange cheese, cut into 8 triangles, over top in a wagon spoke pattern. Broil until cheese is bubbly—about 5 minutes.

Serve with a green salad and bread sticks.

HOMINY BAKE
(SERVES FOUR)

It was a tradition in pioneer days to feed the man who passed your door, no matter who he was, where he had been, what he had done, or where he was going. The West then was full of space, and there were long, lonely stretches from one solitary cabin on the prairie to the next. There were no handy cafés to drop into for a quick bite to eat, and homesteaders unquestioningly offered a place at their table and hay in the barn to riders who passed through. Sometimes it was tough to make a dinner or to stretch one, and this recipe was one my grandmother invented in such an unexpected situation.

1½   *pounds hamburger*
1   *onion, peeled and chopped*
½   *cup chopped celery*
1½   *teaspoons salt*
¼   *teaspoon pepper*
¼   *teaspoon garlic powder*
      pinch oregano
1   *8-oz. can tomato sauce, refilled ½ full with water*
1   *#2½ can hominy, drained*

In a skillet gently brown meat with onion, celery, salt, pepper, garlic powder, and oregano. Stir in tomato sauce, water, and hominy. Pour into an ovenproof casserole and bake at 350° F. for 1 hour. (Although this recipe doesn't call for cheese, it is a good place to use up all those hard, dried out, tag ends of cheese that are lurking around in the refrigerator. Just stir them into the casserole before baking and let them melt into the sauce.)

Serve with carrot and apple salad and BAKED FRUIT COCKTAIL.

HAMBURGER SURPRISE
(SERVES FOUR TO SIX)

This is a lazy cook's invention. Now that I've labeled it, I can't tell who in my family invented it. If I did, I would be unpopular at family reunions—if I ever attend any.

HAMBURGER SURPRISE is a good recipe because it is filling and nutritious, but the best thing about it is that it takes a bit of initial preparation and then leaves the cook free.

1½   pounds hamburger
1   large onion, peeled and sliced
1   #303 can cream-style corn
1   large potato, pared and thinly sliced
3   stalks celery, sliced diagonally
1   #303 can tomatoes, mashed
½   cup buttered bread crumbs
     salt and pepper

Press hamburger evenly in bottom of greased casserole. Layer remaining ingredients into casserole in the order given, seasoning each layer lightly with salt and pepper as you go. Bake at 350° F. for 1 hour.

Make the menu effortless by serving the casserole with a previously made, brightly colored jello salad, and a dessert such as baked apples that cooks while the casserole does. (No messy cleanup chore with this recipe, either!)

SPANISH CASSEROLE
(SERVES FOUR, WITH LEFTOVERS)

Spanish blood flows through the veins of California. Everybody knows that golden state once belonged to Spain, and the warm, rhythmic Spanish names of towns ripple off the tongue: Los Angeles, City of Angels . . . La Jolla . . . Vallejo . . . San Rafael . . . San Francisco . . . San Anselmo . . . San Gabriel . . . Santa Monica . . . Sausalito . . . San Diego. Mexico is just over the border, and the sun of Spain is a taste in the mouth.

1½   pounds hamburger
1   onion, peeled and chopped
1   #303 can tomatoes, mashed
1   can whole kernel corn, drained
1   8-oz. can tomato sauce
2   teaspoons salt
½   teaspoon pepper
2   teaspoons chili powder
½   cup yellow cornmeal
1   cup pitted olives

Lightly brown meat with onion in a large skillet. Add tomatoes, corn, tomato sauce, salt, pepper, and chili powder. Cook 30 minutes over low heat. Add cornmeal and olives and mix well. (If too dry, add a small amount of tomato juice or water.) Transfer to a casserole dish. Bake in a 350° F. oven for 45 minutes, or until lightly browned on top.

Serve with fruit salad and APPLE CRUNCH.

MEXICAN CASSEROLE
(SERVES FOUR TO SIX)

At the waning of winter when I'm tired of snow and warm clothing, I sometimes dream wild dreams of strolling casually into a cantina in Mexico —dressed in something completely unlike anything I ever wear, such as a backless cotton sun dress, barefoot sandals, and a white picture hat—and listening to guitars playing love music while a handsome, dark-eyed man gazes romantically into my eyes. Unfortunately, the handsomest, darkest-eyed Mexican man I've ever known was a dentist who was about as romantic as a fence post. His sister made the basis for this casserole. It isn't especially romantic either, but it tastes good.

1½	*pounds hamburger*
1	*onion, peeled and chopped*
2	*teaspoons salt*
¼	*teaspoon pepper*
1	*tablespoon chili powder*
1	*8-oz. can tomato sauce*
12	*tortillas (cornmeal, not flour)*
1	*4½-oz. can ripe, pitted olives, chopped*
2	*cups grated mild cheddar cheese*
1	*cup hot water*

Brown meat with onion in a skillet. Add seasonings and tomato sauce. In a casserole alternate layers of tortillas (overlapping), meat sauce, a sprinkle of olives, and cheese. Add water and cover. Bake in a hot (400° F.) oven for 20 minutes. Cut into wedges to serve. This may be put together in advance and baked just before serving; but if you do make it in advance, add the water just before baking.

PAISANO CASSEROLE
(SERVES SIX)

The Italian restaurants in San Francisco are superb. The fine, famed restaurants are a gourmet experience, and little, four-table family operations serve splendid food with a robust red wine—and with an attitude of such gregarious delight that you feel they're really glad you came. I had dinner every Monday night for weeks at one neighborhood Italian restaurant until I had figured out this recipe closely enough so that I was satisfied with it.

3   *quarts mashed potatoes (Instant potatoes are cheaper and work well—use a 16-oz. package and prepare according to package directions.)*
6   *cups flour*
1   *teaspoon salt*
1   *teaspoon baking powder*
1   *pound hamburger*
1   *onion, peeled and chopped*
3   *8-oz. cans tomato sauce*
    tomato sauce can filled once with water
    salt to taste
¼   *teaspoon pepper*
¼   *teaspoon oregano*
¼   *teaspoon garlic powder*
1   *cup shredded Monterey Jack cheese*

Mix first 4 ingredients into a firm dough. Roll out by teaspoons into oblong shapes and drop into a kettle of rapidly boiling water. Cook about 15 minutes, or until these "dumplings" rise to the top. Remove and drain.

Make a sauce by lightly browning hamburger with onion until onion is tender. Add tomato sauce, water, and seasonings. Layer dumplings, sauce, and cheese into a casserole and bake in a preheated 350° F. oven for 30 minutes.

Serve with a crisp salad and a light dessert.

VIVA CASSEROLE
(SERVES FOUR TO SIX)

This is one of my favorite recipes, but I have been making it for so long that I cannot remember if it came from someplace or if it just grew. I do remember serving it one time at Lake Tahoe when Tom, my husband, came in with a group of our friends after a glorious day of skiing. Everyone was hungry, and when I brought the casserole in, the whole bunch yelled "Viva!" and gave the dish the name we've called it by since.

1½	*pounds hamburger*
1	*small onion, peeled and chopped*
1	*1¼-oz. package taco seasoning mix*
1	*cup water*
½	*cup bottled taco sauce*
10	*corn tortillas*
2	*packages (10 oz. each) frozen chopped spinach, thawed*
2	*cups shredded Monterey Jack cheese*
1	*cup sour cream*

Brown hamburger and onion in a skillet, stirring meat frequently so it will crumble. Stir in taco seasoning mix and water. Cover and simmer 10 minutes. Pour ¼ cup taco sauce into a 3-quart casserole. Turn 5 corn tortillas in the sauce to coat them lightly, and then arrange them, overlapping, in the bottom of the dish. Press out most of the liquid from the spinach and stir half of it into the hamburger. Spoon half the meat mixture over the tortillas in the casserole and sprinkle with ½ cup cheese. Repeat layers of taco sauce, 5 tortillas, meat, and cheese. Spread top with sour cream, scatter the remaining spinach over it, and sprinkle with remaining cheese. Bake in a 375° F. oven, covered, for 25 minutes. Remove cover and continue baking 25 minutes longer. All you need with this dish is a salad.

EITHER-OR CASSEROLE
(SERVES FOUR)

I have a fondness for easygoing, adaptable recipes which manage to make do quite well with substitutions that are just sitting around in the refrigerator. They're so *liveable.*

This recipe was born high on the Continental Divide where a narrow dirt road crosses between Idaho and Montana at Lemhi Pass. A tiny spring is there, green and merry and rimmed with yellow wildflowers. The sweet water of the spring trickles eastward into Montana and is encouraged by other streams until, when it is all grown up, it has become the Missouri River.

1	*pound hamburger*
1	*onion, peeled and chopped*
1	*teaspoon salt*
¼	*teaspoon pepper*
1	*tablespoon chili powder*
1	*tablespoon vinegar*
1	*teaspoon sugar*
1	*8½-oz. (buffet size) can whole kernel corn*
1	*8-oz. can tomato sauce, refilled ½ full with water*
½	*cup shredded cheddar cheese*

ONE OF THE FOLLOWING:

1	*#303 can (or 2 cups) chili beans;* OR
2	*cups leftover macaroni and cheese;* OR
2	*cups leftover spaghetti in sauce*

In a skillet brown meat and onion. Add seasonings, vinegar, and sugar. Stir in EITHER chili OR macaroni and cheese OR spaghetti. Add corn and tomato sauce and blend. Top with cheese. Simmer slowly 20 minutes.

Serve with a salad and thickly sliced bread.

ITALIAN SAUCE

(SERVES SIX)

I use the same basic sauce for both spaghetti and lasagne, for reasons of economy as well as ease of preparation. The main differences between the two dishes are the pasta, and, of course, the cheeses, which are used in lasagne but not in spaghetti. However, as far as the basic sauce is concerned, this one will do nobly for both.

1½   *pounds hamburger*
1   *onion, peeled and chopped*
2   *stalks celery, chopped*
1   *green pepper, chopped*
1   *8-oz. can mushrooms, or 8 fresh mushrooms, sliced*
1   *6-oz. can pitted ripe olives, sliced (optional)*
1   *#303 can tomatoes, mashed*
2   *8-oz. cans tomato sauce, with 1 refilled with water*
1   *clove garlic, crushed*
¼   *teaspoon oregano*
¼   *teaspoon marjoram*
¼   *teaspoon basil*
¼   *teaspoon rosemary*
1   *small bay leaf*
       salt to taste

Lightly brown hamburger in a large, heavy kettle, stirring until it is crumbly. Add onion and celery, and simmer gently 5 minutes. Add remaining ingredients. Simmer very gently, covered, for at least 2 hours. Add water or, preferably, tomato juice if the sauce gets too thick. Taste and readjust seasonings about ½ hour before serving.

If you have a cup of leftover brown gravy, do stir it in when you add the tomato sauce. It adds a superlative touch to the sauce. So does ½ cup of any kind of red or pink wine, added during the last hour of simmering.

FOR SPAGHETTI

Long strand spaghetti is best in my opinion, but use the type you prefer. Gently drop spaghetti into briskly boiling water to which you have added

1 tablespoon oil and 1 teaspoon salt. Cook until spaghetti is just tender, but not soggy. Drain immediately. Bring ⅓ cup cooking or olive oil or melted margarine to a fast simmer (just under the boiling point), then pour over drained spaghetti, turning and tossing until spaghetti is well coated. Pour sauce over individual plates of spaghetti and sprinkle with grated Parmesan or Romano cheese.

FOR LASAGNE

1	*16-oz. package lasagne pasta*
1	*tablespoon oil*
1	*teaspoon salt*
1	*recipe Italian Sauce*
1	*cup ricotta or dry cottage cheese*
8	*or 9 slices mozzarella or Monterey Jack cheese*
1½	*cups shredded mild cheddar cheese*

Cook lasagne pasta according to package directions, or in briskly boiling water to which you have added 1 tablespoon oil and 1 teaspoon salt. Cook until lasagne is tender, but not soggy. Drain well. Gently arrange a layer of lasagne in the bottom of a large roasting pan, one strip at a time. Spread layer evenly with sauce. Top with a thin layer of ricotta or dry cottage cheese, a layer of thinly sliced mozzarella or Monterey Jack cheese, and a layer of shredded mild cheddar. Repeat layers until all ingredients are used up, with cheese layer on top. Bake, covered, in a 350° F. oven for 30 minutes. Remove cover and bake an additional 20 minutes or until top is bubbly and lightly browned. Slice in squares and serve with crusty garlic bread and a green salad.

BURRITOS

My husband likes burritos because he was born in the Southwest and ate them with gusto there. I like them not only because they taste good but also because they are a nifty hidey-hole for odd dabs of leftovers, without betraying to anybody that they are leftovers.

Start by buying a dozen flour tortillas, or by making your own.

FLOUR TORTILLAS

4   *cups all-purpose flour*
2   *teaspoons salt*
⅓   *cup shortening or lard*
4   *teaspoons baking powder*
1   *cup warm water—more, if needed*

Work first 4 ingredients together, then add enough water to form into a ball. Knead. Let set 30 minutes. Form into balls the size of a large egg. Roll out, on a lightly floured board, until they are round and very thin and about 12 inches in diameter. Cook quickly on a hot, ungreased skillet or griddle— about 2 minutes on one side, then turn and cook about 1 minute on the second side.

They keep frozen very well. To reheat after freezing, or to heat store-bought tortillas, put about ⅔ cup water in the bottom of a skillet or electric frying pan. Place a foil-covered rack in the skillet and stack tortillas on the rack. Cover and steam for a few minutes.

Serve the flour tortillas sometimes simply heated and buttered, in place of ordinary bread. They are delicious with a tart jelly spread on them.

BURRITO FILLING

1½   *pounds hamburger or 3 cups leftover cubed meat—beef roast, ham, lamb, meatloaf, chicken, or turkey*
1   *onion, peeled and chopped*
1   *large stalk celery, chopped*
1   *green pepper, chopped*
     salt to taste
¼   *teaspoon pepper*
¼   *teaspoon garlic powder*
¼   *teaspoon marjoram*
½   *teaspoon sugar*
2   *8-oz. cans tomato sauce or 2 cups tomato juice*
1½   *to 2 cups one of the following OR a mixture of two or more: chili beans; leftover macaroni and cheese; leftover spaghetti or lasagne; leftover stew*

Gently brown hamburger with onion, celery, and green pepper. Add remaining ingredients and simmer gently 20 minutes. (Add 1 cup of any leftover cheese you have in the refrigerator, if the idea appeals to you, and simmer 5 minutes, stirring, until cheese has melted.) Mixture should be fairly thick.

Heat tortillas. (See instructions for heating in FLOUR TORTILLAS recipe.) Place a heated tortilla on a flat surface near your skillet of filling. At one end of each tortilla place 1/3 to 1/2 cup of meat mixture. Roll up evenly and put in baking dish. Keep completed burritos hot as you go. When all burritos are made, pour any remaining filling mixture over them or butter the tops with a lavish hand and, perhaps, sprinkle with grated cheese.

Serve hot, with a fruit salad.

TACOS
(SERVES FOUR HEARTY OR SIX AVERAGE EATERS)

Tacos are popular in our house, for everyone likes the zesty little Mexican sandwiches and enjoys the casual, picnic atmosphere of making his own. You can make your own corn tortillas, but they require a special corn flour that is often difficult to find. You *can* work around and substitute cornmeal for part of the white flour in the recipe for flour tortillas. I have tried this, and, frankly, my cornmeal-based corn tortillas were not very good. As long as corn tortillas are sold frozen for about two cents each, I'll buy mine ready-made. There are, doubtless, many excellent recipes for making your own corn tortillas. If there are, I don't want to know about them.

2 *pounds hamburger*
1 *package taco seasoning mix* OR *1½ teaspoons salt, ½ teaspoon pepper, 2 teaspoons chili powder, 1 teaspoon cumin, ¼ teaspoon oregano, and pinch thyme*
¼ *teaspoon garlic powder*
1 *small head lettuce, shredded*
4 *tomatoes, chopped*
2 *or 3 onions, peeled and chopped*
½ *to 1 pound cheddar cheese, shredded*
   hot jalapeno relish or a bottle of taco sauce
   packaged or homemade tortillas

Sauté the hamburger gently in a minimum of hot fat in a large skillet, stirring so it will be crumbly. Season with taco seasoning mix or individual seasonings and garlic powder. Simmer gently and stir occasionally while you prepare the remainder of the taco ingredients.

As you prepare the following, place each in individual serving bowls. Arrange the bowls on the table with a large bowl in the center for the meat mixture and a large platter waiting to receive the tortillas as you fry them. (A towel folded in thirds on the platter is helpful—insert the cooked and folded tortillas in the towel, which will help absorb excessive grease and at the same time will keep the tortillas warm until they are used.) Everyone builds his own taco, piling on the combination of ingredients he likes best.

In individual bowls place: shredded lettuce, chopped tomatoes, chopped onions, and cheese. Place within reach a bowl of hot jalapeno relish or a bottle of taco sauce for individual use.

To fry the tortillas: In a large, heavy skillet heat ½ cup oil. When hot, slide in a tortilla. Wait a few seconds and fold the tortilla in half with the cooked side in. Add a second tortilla. When you fold the second tortilla, turn the first one so the other side cooks. With a little practice—and a pair of kitchen tongs to prevent burned fingers—you can have 3 tortillas going at one time. When each is finished, place it within the folded towel on the platter so it will keep hot.

To make tacos, place in each cooked, folded tortilla first a hefty spoonful of the meat mixture, then a sprinkle of each of the remaining ingredients according to inclination.

Serve with large napkins to wipe dripping chins and fingers, and enjoy, enjoy.

Chapter 3

HAM CAN BE A GOOD INVESTMENT

There was a little canyon in Idaho with an evening breeze, a cabin, five cherry trees, and a view.

We heated with a wood stove and wood we had cut and hauled the old way. Tommy Lee was born on New Year's Eve, and we would pull his cradle near the stove and keep him warm with lodgepole pine, Douglas fir, and quaking aspen that smelled like apples as it burned.

We savored the place names of Idaho—marvelous, colorful names such as Long Tom, Sweat Lake, Bear Trap, Gunbarrel, Wagonhammer, Double Dollar, Grizzly Springs, Tin Cup, and the lovely Silverlead. We had very little money, so we walked and hiked and picnicked and put wild loveliness in our memories to keep forever. We learned the "use it up, wear it out, make it do or do without" philosophy of our far-off neighbors, and from them I learned that a big ham was a good investment for slim budgets. They considered a ham as food for several days, and treated one in successive steps.

FIRST STEP

1   *6- to 8-pound ham or pork shoulder, bone in*
1   *cup fruit syrup (drained from canned fruit—accumulate in a jar*
     and keep refrigerated until needed)
½   *cup brown sugar*
½   *teaspoon dry mustard*
⅓   *to ½ cup raisins*
1   *tablespoon cornstarch*

Bake the ham, uncovered, and do not glaze it. Make a separate sauce out of the cup of syrup, brown sugar, mustard, and raisins. Heat and thicken slightly with cornstarch. Pour over ham slices which have been arranged on a platter.

Serve with baked or scalloped potatoes and a cabbage-apple salad. Depending on the appetites, ⅓ of the ham will serve four to six.

SECOND STEP

Take ⅓ of the remaining ham and put it through the food grinder with sweet pickle and onion. Blend with enough mayonnaise to make a good spreading consistency. This makes a fair amount of excellent sandwich filling.

THIRD STEP

Cut the remaining ham into small chunks. Reserve a cup of these to stir into breakfast scrambled eggs, and use the remainder for either a casserole of potatoes and ham or a hearty HAM AND POTATO SOUP or in one of the following recipes.

FOURTH STEP

You will be left with a ham bone and those trimmings you have saved all along. Look up a ham and beans recipe and make it.

If you have leftover from the ham and beans, push the limit out of the whole process by thinning the leftover to a soup consistency with water; a #303 can of tomatoes, mashed; and seasonings to taste. You'll have a fine luncheon bean soup.

HAM AND POTATO CASSEROLE
(SERVES FOUR)

     about 4 potatoes, peeled
2   *onions, peeled*
2   *to 3 cups ham pieces*
     salt and pepper
     milk
½   *cup grated or shredded cheddar cheese*

Slice potatoes thinly. Spread a layer in a greased casserole dish. Add a layer of sliced onions, then a layer of ham pieces. Repeat layers, seasoning each layer with salt and pepper as you go. End with potatoes. Pour milk to ½ inch from top of dish. Sprinkle top with cheese. Bake at 350° F. for 1 hour, or until potatoes are tender and top is nicely browned.

Serve with a family-favorite salad—one with a jello base is good with this—and a bright vegetable. My family thinks gingerbread, still warm from the oven, is the way to end this economical dinner.

HOLY-TOLEDO HAM
(SERVES FOUR)

2   *cups buttered cracker crumbs (Spread crackers with butter and put together, sandwich style, with buttered sides together, then roll with a rolling pin.)*
4   *hard-cooked eggs, peeled and finely chopped*
1   *large green pepper, finely chopped*
2   *cups medium white sauce*
1½   *cups chopped cooked ham*
     salt and pepper

Sprinkle the bottom of a well-greased casserole dish or baking pan with ¾ cup buttered cracker crumbs. Cover with 2 hard-cooked, finely chopped eggs, and half the chopped green pepper. Sprinkle with 1 cup of white sauce, then half the ham pieces. Season. Repeat layers. Season again and top with ½ cup buttered cracker crumbs. Bake at 375° F. about 20 to 25 minutes.

Serve with CANDY CARROTS, FRUIT SALAD, and biscuits.

HAM DAY-BEFORE-PAYDAY
(SERVES FOUR)

This was a Desperation Dish, created on a day during a lean-money time when I had to come up with an unexpected-company-for-dinner menu, with the added handicap of being thirty-three miles from the nearest market and having no money to buy goodies, even if I had been able to get there. It was so good a dish that we have had it many times since. I usually serve this with tomato casserole and a marinated vegetable plate.

    2   cups cooked macaroni
    1½   to 2 cups finely chopped cooked ham
    ¼   teaspoon pepper
    ½   teaspoon salt
    ¼   cup finely minced, peeled onion
    ½   cup finely minced celery
    2   cups milk
    2   eggs, beaten

Put macaroni in a buttered casserole or baking dish. Cover with 1 cup ham mixed with seasonings, onion, and celery. Sprinkle with remaining ham. Add eggs to milk, beat together, and pour over mixture. Bake in a 350° F. oven until firm, about ½ hour.

HAM AND MACARONI BAKE
(SERVES FOUR)

Serve this dish with brightly colored side dishes. Try a bright green vegetable, or beets, and a tomato aspic.

1	*8-oz. package elbow macaroni, cooked and drained*
1½	*to 2 cups chopped cooked ham*
1½	*cups shredded cheddar or American cheese*
2	*cups medium white sauce*
½	*cup buttered cracker crumbs (Spread crackers with butter before crumbling.)*

Mix macaroni with ham. Make medium white sauce and stir in 1 cup shredded cheese. Arrange half the ham mixture in a buttered casserole. Pour over half of the cheese mixture. Repeat. Sprinkle the top with remaining cheese and buttered crumbs. Bake in a 350° F. oven until browned—15 to 20 minutes.

Chapter 4

CHICKEN— EVERYBODY'S FAVORITE WAY TO MAKE A FOOD BUDGET WORK

If hamburger is the backbone of the average grocery budget, chicken must be the arms and legs. Buy it whole and cut it up yourself to save money, and try it different ways for the sake of variety.

BEST-EVER FRIED CHICKEN

(SERVES FOUR—BARELY)

My family can't make up its collective mind whether it likes this chicken piping hot at the time of serving, or later, cold, for snacks or picnics. Start out with it hot as part of a "See America First" dinner, served with mashed potatoes and pan gravy, whole kernel corn or corn on the cob, and apple pie.

  1 *large fryer, cut up*
     flour for dredging
     salt and pepper
     ground sage or poultry seasoning
     garlic powder

Dredge chicken in flour and brown in hot fat over medium heat. When one side is nicely golden, turn and season the browned side with salt, pepper, a timid shake of sage or poultry seasoning, and a confident shake of garlic powder. When the second side is golden, reduce heat and cook slowly until chicken starts to get tender inside and crispy outside. Turn and season again. Continue cooking slowly until done—about 1 hour. Remove chicken pieces to a warm platter and keep hot.

CHICKEN PAN GRAVY

     about 3 tablespoons flour
  2 *cups milk*
  1 *cup water*
     salt and pepper

Scrape skillet in which chicken has cooked to loosen bits of chicken. Stir in flour and blend well with the pan drippings over medium heat. Slowly pour in milk mixed with water, stirring constantly. Season to taste with salt and pepper, and continue to simmer 5 minutes, stirring. Add more water or milk if you like a thinner gravy.

For fewer calories and a happier cholesterol situation—without sacrificing taste appeal—pull the skin off the chicken (except for the wings, which is impossible) before dredging in flour and cook the chicken skinless.

If you allow the floured pieces to set for several minutes before cooking them, you will still have a delicious crust and the seasonings will penetrate the meat even better than when the skin is left on. Put the discarded skin, the neck, and the wing tips in a saucepan with water to cover by an inch or two, and simmer 1 hour. Strain. This broth is good for soup stock, "gravy makings," or vegetable seasoning.

CREAMED BAKED CHICKEN
(SERVES FOUR)

Sage must be the smell of the West, coming on the wind off lonely sagebrush prairies where wagons once rolled, carrying dreamers to their dreams. In spring, sage land is purple with the misty little blossoms; and in winter, wild things exist on a diet of sage.

The sage used in kitchens is a different variety, although I've added an ordinary sagebrush leaf to many a campfire stew. Coffee brewed in my old blackened coffee pot over skimpy sagebrush fires has a special taste, although whether the taste of sage smoke or the setting makes the difference I'm not prepared to decide.

In this recipe, from the sagebrush prairies of the West, sage, ground and provided in tidy little cans and bottles, makes a difference.

1   *large fryer, cut into serving pieces*
1½   *teaspoon salt*
¼   *teaspoon pepper*
¼   *teaspoon ground sage*
1   *cup evaporated milk or 1½ cups cream*

Dredge chicken pieces in flour. Place in well-greased roasting pan and season. Dilute evaporated milk with ½ cup water, or use undiluted cream, and pour over chicken. Cover and bake at 350° F. for 1 hour. Remove cover and bake 15 minutes longer.

Serve with whipped potatoes and butter, CRUNCHY SALAD, and a fruit pie.

CHIP CHICKEN
(SERVES FOUR)

The flavor appeal of this chicken is in the tangy crust. Make it better—and better for your cholesterol level—by pulling the skin from the pieces before coating with chips and egg mixture.

1   *large fryer, cut into serving pieces*
1   *small package fresh potato chips*
2   *eggs, beaten*
⅓   *cup milk*
½   *cup butter or margarine*

Roll potato chips with a rolling pin until you have 1½ to 2 cups chip crumbs. Combine eggs and milk in a flat pan. Melt butter and pour into a shallow baking dish. Dip chicken pieces first in chips, then in egg mixture, then again in chips. Put pieces in melted butter in baking dish. Cover and bake at 350° F. for 45 minutes. Remove cover and bake an additional 10 minutes, or until chicken has turned a golden brown.
     Serve with fried rice and fresh fruit salad.

DIP CHICKEN
(SERVES FOUR)

This chicken is flavorful and pretty enough to make as a "company dinner" entrée, but it is easy enough to serve for a busy day family dinner.

1   *large fryer, cut into serving pieces*
2   *packages onion soup mix*
1   *pint plain yogurt*
½   *cup butter or margarine*

Empty onion soup mix into a flat dish, such as a pie pan. Mash out lumps. Add yogurt and stir well to blend. Melt butter in a shallow baking dish or casserole. Dip chicken pieces in dip, coating heavily, and arrange in baking dish. Cover and bake at 350° F. for 45 minutes. Remove cover and bake an additional 15 minutes.

Serve with a lettuce and tomato salad and, as long as you will be using your oven anyway, baked potatoes; or with baked squash dribbled with honey, and coleslaw.

OVEN-BARBECUED CHICKEN
(SERVES FOUR)

I always serve this with hot, buttered rice and a CANARY ISLANDS SALAD. This recipe was created high in the Sierra Nevada Mountains, in a happy house near a lake of such beauty that it is still total in my eyes. I remember, back through the twelve years that separate now from then, the first time that I cooked this chicken and served it to the magic of Rachmaninoff's Second Piano Concerto. We licked sauce from our fingers, listened to music and the lake, and felt good about ourselves, each other, and the whole world.

1   *large chicken, cut into serving pieces*
1   *8-oz. can tomato sauce*
1/4 *cup cooking oil*
1/3 *cup vinegar*
1   *cup cola (soft drink) or stale beer*
1   *cup brown sugar*
1/2 *teaspoon garlic powder*
1/4 *teaspoon oregano*
1   *teaspoon whole rosemary*

Brown chicken, without flouring, in hot fat. Arrange in a baking dish or casserole. Combine remaining ingredients and blend well, stirring out lumps of brown sugar. Pour over chicken pieces, getting sauce under chicken as well as over it. Cover and bake at 350° F. for 45 minutes, turning occasionally in the sauce. Uncover and continue baking 20 minutes.

Serve with love.

SMOTHERED CHICKEN
(SERVES FOUR AMPLY)

1	*large fryer or stewing hen, cut into serving pieces*
	flour for dredging
1½	*teaspoons salt*
½	*teaspoon garlic powder*
¼	*teaspoon sage*
¼	*teaspoon pepper*
	water
3	*potatoes, peeled and quartered*
1	*large onion, peeled, cut into thick slices*

Serve this with a three-bean salad and buttery biscuits or hot rolls. It is important to remove skin from the chicken in this recipe—from all but the wings—especially if you are using a tougher stewing hen instead of a tender fryer.

Dredge chicken heavily in flour and brown in hot fat in a deep, heavy skillet that has a tightly fitting lid. When chicken has browned well on both sides, season with mixed-together seasonings. Cover with hot water. Put lid on skillet and cook over low heat for 30 minutes. Remove lid and gently lift out chicken. Stir bottom of skillet to loosen crusty bits. Add potatoes and onions. Arrange chicken pieces on top. Re-season, if necessary, and add water to just touch the sides of the chicken. Cover again and simmer gently until potatoes are tender—about 30 minutes.

CHICKEN WITH NOODLES OR DUMPLINGS
(SERVES FOUR HEARTILY)

Chicken and noodles or chicken and dumplings are "native" to the whole country, not just to any of its parts. This is the way we do it where I live, served with cabbage salad, hot buttered beets, and light rolls on the side for sly dunking in the gravy.

1	*4- or 5-pound stewing hen, cut into serving pieces*
1	*large onion, peeled and chopped*
2	*stalks celery, chopped*
	water
1½	*teaspoons salt*
¼	*teaspoon pepper*
¼	*teaspoon oregano*
¼	*teaspoon paprika*
3	*cups uncooked egg noodles or 1 recipe dumpling dough*

Place chicken pieces in deep kettle and cover with water. Add onions and celery. Simmer gently, covered, 45 minutes to an hour or until chicken is tender. Add seasonings and additional hot water to bring the water back to its original level. Stir in noodles, or heat to boiling and drop spoonsful of dumpling dough on top. Cover tightly and continue simmering until done—20 to 30 minutes.

PARTY ROAST CHICKEN
(SERVES FOUR)

Serve this with rice, mashed potatoes, or noodles, to receive the gravy. Add a plate of vegetables—cooked, marinated, or chilled—with onion-flavored bread sticks.

1   *whole chicken*
1   *recipe bread dressing (recipe in Chapter 7, "Potatoes and Other Fillers")*
1   *stick butter or margarine*
    water
3   *tablespoons flour*
    salt to taste
¼   *teaspoon pepper*

Rub chicken cavity with margarine and sprinkle lightly with salt. Stuff with dressing. Rub outside of chicken liberally with margarine. Cover with foil and roast in a 325° F. oven about 1 hour. Remove foil and continue cooking until chicken has browned well—20 to 30 minutes. Remove chicken to platter and keep hot. Put roasting pan on stove-top burner. Loosen drippings and add 2½ to 3 cups hot water. Bring to a boil. In a jar with a tightly fitting lid put flour and ⅔ cup water. Shake hard until mixture is smooth. Pour slowly into boiling gravy water, stirring constantly. Simmer until thickened, seasoning with salt and pepper.

BERNIE'S CHICKEN
(SERVES FOUR)

Bernie is a friend—creative, gregarious, opinionated, stubborn, and possessed of a lavish Texan hospitality. It makes me nervous to cook for him because he is just as noisy about something that doesn't suit him as he is about something he likes. He will never know that I once bought a cheese cake mix and passed it off as my own. I serve this chicken to him often because he loves it and I know it's foolproof. Many people have a friend like Bernie, and it is reassuring to have a recipe like this to rely on.

1   *large fryer, whole*
      margarine or butter, about ½ cup
1½   *cups brown, unprocessed, uncooked rice*
2   *tablespoons soy sauce*
2   *green onions, chopped, with tops*
8   *fresh mushrooms, sliced*

Bring 3 cups lightly salted water to a boil. Add rice, reduce heat to a slow simmer, and cover pan. Cook until all water is absorbed and rice is barely tender—45 minutes to an hour. Turn cooked rice into a skillet in which you have melted ¼ cup butter or margarine. Add soy sauce, onions, and mushrooms. Stir to mix well, turn off heat, and let rice sit for 5 minutes.

Put whole chicken in a well-greased roasting pan. Stuff chicken with rice mixture, and pile remaining rice closely around chicken. Dot bits of butter over chicken and rice. Cover closely with foil and roast at 350° F. for 1½ hours. Remove foil and continue roasting until chicken is browned.

Serve with hot rolls and a big green salad.

Chapter 5

FISH—THE NO WASTE WAY TO START A MEAL

Fish for dinner arrives with impressive recommendations. It's economical, for one thing, because there is very little waste. It's highly nutritious, too, providing a high mineral salt content in addition to goodly quantities of iron, copper, iodine, and vitamins A and D—so you get a lot for your money. And it's good to eat.

Fish advertised as "drawn" or "dressed" is whole and ready-to-cook, with entrails removed. (The head, fins, and tail may or may not be removed.) Steaks are cross-section cuts, usually ¾-inch to 1-inch thick. Fillets are cuts off the side of the fish, lengthwise pieces that are boneless. Sticks are oblong pieces of fish cut from fillets and steaks or lesser quality cuts of fish, and are usually breaded.

In figuring quantities, ⅓ pound fillets, steaks, or sticks will be sufficient for one person; ½ pound per person is required for dressed or drawn fish; and 1½ pounds of headless frozen or fresh shrimp will serve four to six. If you buy oysters and clams in the shell, 3 dozen will feed six people; shucked, a quart will feed six.

FISH PIQUANT

(SERVES FOUR TO SIX)

This zesty dish is elegant enough for company dinners. Serve with a cucumber salad, baked potatoes, and a bright vegetable.

4   *onions, peeled and sliced*
2   *pounds fish fillets—cod, sole, haddock, mackerel, salmon, snapper, or whitefish*
½   *cup mayonnaise*
1   *tablespoon Worcestershire sauce*
3   *tablespoons lemon juice*
⅓   *cup grated Parmesan cheese*
2   *tablespoons finely minced celery*
2   *tablespoons finely chopped parsley*

Slice 4 onions, cover with water, and simmer until slices are tender but still crispy. Drain and spread in a shallow, well-greased casserole or baking pan. Cut fish fillets into individual serving pieces and place over the onions. Combine remaining ingredients and blend well. Spread mixture over fish. Bake at 350° F. for 30 minutes, or until fish flakes easily when pierced with a fork.

BAKED FISH FILLETS

(SERVES FOUR)

This is one of those sophisticated-but-simple recipes that calls for sophisticated-but-simple accompaniments, and is suited to one of those candlelit scenes where your guests go away talking about you and your elegant little dinners.

Serve with cooked, chilled artichokes and melted butter; brown rice cooked to the chewy stage and then sautéed with minced green onions; and baked oranges dribbled with honey for dessert. No one would guess how easy the menu is.

12   fresh mushrooms, sliced, or 1 6-oz. can sliced mushrooms, drained
¼   cup butter or margarine
1   small onion, peeled and minced
½   green pepper, chopped finely
1   stalk celery, chopped finely
2   teaspoons salt
½   teaspoon basil
¼   teaspoon garlic powder
2   1-pound fish fillets
¼   cup shredded Swiss or Monterey Jack cheese

Slice mushrooms or drain canned mushrooms. Sauté in ¼ cup melted butter with onion, green pepper, celery, 1 teaspoon salt, and seasonings until onion is golden. Sprinkle fish with 1 teaspoon salt. Place 1 fillet in baking dish. Spread sautéed mixture over fish. Lay second fillet over top and sprinkle with cheese. Dot with butter. Bake at 400° F. for 20 minutes, reduce heat to 300° F., and bake 15 minutes longer.

QUEEN CHARLOTTE FISH
(SERVES FOUR OR FIVE)

People who live along seacoasts know what to do with fish. This fine recipe is adapted from one I tasted in the lovely Queen Charlotte Islands of British Columbia. I like to serve it with rice and a green salad, and fruit for dessert.

2   pounds fish fillets
2½   teaspoons salt
     pepper
     about 2 tablespoons lemon juice
6   tablespoons butter or margarine
4   tablespoons flour
1   cup milk
2   egg yolks
4   tablespoons grated Parmesan or cheddar cheese

Place fish fillets in a buttered, shallow 1½-quart baking dish. Sprinkle with 1 teaspoon salt, pepper, lemon juice, and dot with 1 tablespoon butter. Cover with foil and bake at 350° F. for 20 minutes. Heat 2 tablespoons butter in saucepan over low heat; blend in flour, 1½ teaspoon salt, dash pepper. Heat until mixture just starts to bubble. Remove from heat and gradually add milk, stirring constantly. Cook rapidly, stirring constantly, until sauce thickens. Cook for 1 minute. Blend in egg yolks and 3 tablespoons butter. Drain excess liquid from fish; cover with sauce. Sprinkle with cheese. Broil 4 to 5 inches from heat for 2 minutes, or until fish is golden.

FLATHEAD FISH

(SERVES FOUR)

Flathead Lake is one of Montana's jewels, shimmering through a rim of cherry trees, with the Mission Mountains marching grandly off to the east and the Salish Mountains rolling westward. Osprey build scraggly stick nests in the tops of dead trees on many of the lake's islands, and roam the sky like fierce kites. The lake is on the Flathead Indian reservation, and it gets its name from them. Friends served this fine dinner to us there—with escalloped potatoes, a green vegetable, and cherry cobbler to go with the fish.

2   *pounds fish fillets*
1   *egg, slightly beaten*
⅓   *cup soft bread crumbs*
3   *tomatoes, halved*
     salt
     pepper
¼   *cup finely chopped, peeled onion*
12   *fresh mushrooms, sliced*
¼   *cup butter or margarine, melted*
¼   *cup grated cheddar cheese*

Place fillets on a greased, flat baking dish. Spread beaten egg over fish. Sprinkle with bread crumbs. Garnish with tomato halves. Season over all with salt and pepper to taste. Fry onion and mushrooms in melted butter until onion is golden. Spread evenly over fish. Sprinkle fish and tomatoes with cheese. Bake at 350° F. for 25 minutes.

FANCY FISH
(SERVES FOUR)

I found this recipe—quick, easy, inexpensive, and good—a thousand miles from the nearest seacoast, proving that quick-freeze methods make fish available for everybody.

2 *pounds fish fillets*
4 *eggs*
1 *teaspoon allspice*
1 *clove garlic, finely minced*
2 *tablespoons milk or cream*
  salt and pepper
  cooking oil
2 *tablespoons butter or margarine*
1 *teaspoon finely chopped parsley*
1 *tablespoon lemon juice*

Beat eggs with allspice, garlic, and milk until frothy. Rub salt and pepper into fish fillets. Soak fillets in egg mixture for 30 minutes. Fry fillets in hot oil until flaky—I have best luck when I get the oil hot, then reduce heat to low and add the fish—cooking them 7 to 10 minutes on one side, depending on the thickness of the fillets, then turning and cooking them 5 minutes longer.

Remove fish from skillet. To the pan juices add butter, parsley, and lemon juice. Heat, stirring, and pour sauce over fish fillets.

Serve with hot buttered rice and a fruit salad.

FAMILY FILLETS
(SERVES FOUR)

This cheap-and-easy recipe is a family standby, as it is gentle on the budget and takes next to nothing in preparation time. Keep the entire menu cheap-and-easy by serving sliced tomatoes, steamed broccoli, and ice cream sundaes for dessert.

1½   *to 2 pounds fish fillets*
     salt and pepper
     Worcestershire sauce
1   *egg, beaten*
½   *cup buttered cracker crumbs (½ cup cracker crumbs to which*
     1 tablespoon melted butter has been added and stirred well)

Lay fillets on oiled aluminum foil on a cookie sheet. Season with salt, pepper, and several shakes of Worcestershire sauce. Beat egg and spread over fish. Sprinkle with buttered crumbs. Bake in a 450° F. oven 15 minutes, or until juice bubbles from the thickest part of the fish.

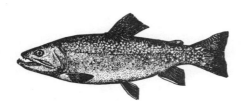

SUPREME FILLETS
(SERVES FOUR)

The tasty breaded coating on these fillets turns a pretty golden color during the baking and adds eye-appeal to taste-appeal. I like to serve a spicy vegetable, such as BEETS HARVARD, and fruit salad with this dish.

1½   *to 2 pounds fish fillets*
¼   *cup evaporated milk mixed with ¼ cup water*
2   *teaspoons salt*
     a hearty dash of garlic powder
2   *cups fine bread crumbs*
2   *tablespoons cooking oil*

Mix milk and water with salt and garlic powder. Dip fillets first in milk mixture and then in bread crumbs, until they are thickly coated. Place on shallow, oiled baking dish. Drizzle with cooking oil. Preheat oven to 500° F. and bake fish for 10 minutes.

LIMEHOUSE FISH
(SERVES FOUR OR FIVE)

This fish dish looks so nice everyone will think you spent time and effort preparing it. Yet it takes next to no time and requires little effort. Serve it with baked potatoes and a tossed green salad to keep the menu effortless and inexpensive.

> 2 *large fish fillets—about 1 pound each*
> *juice of two limes*
> *mayonnaise*
> *paprika, salt, and pepper*

Oil aluminum foil well, turning up edges to make a rim so juices will not run off. Place foil in baking dish or on cookie sheet, then place fillets on foil. With a sharp knife score the fish in a crisscross pattern and dribble lime juice over. Let stand 30 minutes. Preheat broiler. Spread tops of fish with mayonnaise. Place pan 5 inches from heat and broil 5 minutes, or until mayonnaise bubbles and browns. Sprinkle with paprika, salt, and pepper.

SIMPLE SIMON FISH
(SERVES FOUR)

Our family, probably like yours, keeps a busy schedule. My husband is an outdoor and wildlife photographer who works crazy hours; our oldest son is in college and often brings friends home; and I try to keep up with a large log house, a seven-year-old boy, a hectic writing schedule, a horse, two dogs, three cats, one cantankerous pet goose, and a continuous houseful of friends who drop by. Recipes like this help me keep my sanity and maintain my preciously held illusion that I am a good cook.

> 1½ *to 2 pounds fish fillets or steaks*
> *salt and pepper*
> *garlic powder*
> *mayonnaise*
> 12 *saltine crackers, rolled into fine crumbs*

Lay fish on oiled foil on a cookie sheet. Sprinkle with salt, pepper, and a whiff of garlic powder. Spread thickly with mayonnaise. Sprinkle cracker crumbs evenly over fish. Bake in a 400° F. oven for 15 minutes, or until mayonnaise bubbles and turns golden brown.

I serve this dish with either baked potatoes or hot buttered rice, a tossed green salad, and hot rolls that go from freezer to oven to plate.

FOUR WAYS WITH SALMON

I have lived on the West coast, near the Sacramento River and by the Salmon River, and have camped on the British Columbia coast. I have learned to love salmon—fresh, frozen, leftover, or canned. These are my favorite ways of cooking it.

SALMON STEAKS
(SERVES FOUR)

Fresh salmon has become so frightfully expensive that this recipe is really affordable only for those who live near waters where salmon run—where the price is generally much lower or where they can catch their own.

4   *salmon steaks*
     flour seasoned with salt, pepper, garlic powder, paprika, and a whiff of basil
½   *cup white wine*
1   *cup sour cream blended with 1 teaspoon paprika*
     butter

Dredge steaks in flour and sauté in butter until done. Remove from skillet and keep warm. To the pan juices add wine and cook, stirring, until reduced to ¼ cup. Stir in sour cream blended with paprika. Heat but do not boil. Pour over fish.

Serve with baked potatoes, broccoli or asparagus spears, and a salad of mixed fresh fruit.

SALMON LOAF
(SERVES FOUR)

The touch of sage in this recipe is a surprise, and makes it different from any other salmon loaf recipe. Serve this with baked potatoes and a tomato casserole so that the entire dinner cooks in the oven at the same time.

Since in this recipe a pound of salmon goes a long way, the use of dreadfully expensive salmon becomes much more realistic.

½ *cup buttered soft bread crumbs*
2   *eggs, slightly beaten*
½ *cup milk*
1   *1-pound can salmon, flaked, or the same amount of leftover cooked salmon*
1   *tablespon lemon juice*
1   *teaspoon salt*
    dash pepper
½ *teaspoon sage*
3   *tablespoons finely minced, peeled onion*
2   *tablespoons finely chopped celery*
3   *tablespoons melted butter or margarine*

Combine all ingredients and mix well together. Pack firmly into a buttered loaf pan and bake at 350° F. for 30 minutes.

PLANKED SALMON
(SERVES FOUR)

The expense of salmon in this recipe is justified because the dish is almost a complete dinner in itself. You need add only a salad.

1   *1-pound can salmon, removed whole and cut into quarters, or leftover cooked salmon pressed into 4 1½-inch thick patties*
¼   *cup evaporated milk or cream*
2   *cups mashed potatoes—about 4 medium potatoes*
    salt and pepper
    pinch of basil
2   *slices bacon, diced*
1   *medium onion, peeled and sliced*
1   *can french-cut string beans, or 1 can whole kernel corn—#303 size of either one*

Place salmon patties in center of a well-oiled baking plank or ovenproof platter. Place in a 350° F. oven about 20 minutes or until salmon is heated through, basting with milk to keep it moist. Season mashed potatoes with salt, pepper, and basil.

Sauté bacon until just crisp. Remove from skillet and add onion to bacon fat. Fry until golden. Return bacon to pan, add can of drained vegetables, and season. Remove salmon from oven. Surround with string beans or corn, then with a circle of mashed potatoes fluffed into peaks. Return to oven and bake 15 minutes, or until potatoes are golden brown.

SALMON WITH SAUCE

(SERVES FOUR WITH HEARTY APPETITES
OR SIX DAINTY EATERS)

1   *cup medium white sauce*

1   *cup grated mild cheddar or American cheese*

1   *egg yolk, beaten*

2   *cups seasoned mashed potatoes—about 4 medium potatoes*

1   *1-pound can salmon, flaked, or the same amount of leftover cooked salmon*

½   *cup cracker crumbs mixed well with 2 tablespoons melted butter or margarine*

Make 1 cup medium white sauce and season to taste with salt and pepper. Add cheese and egg yolk. Place 2 cups mashed potatoes in buttered baking dish and pour half the sauce over the potatoes. Cover first with flaked salmon, then with remaining sauce. Sprinkle with cracker crumbs and bake at 350° F. for 20 minutes, or until piping hot.

As with the preceding canned salmon recipes, the expense of canned salmon is eased because this recipe stretches so far and is almost a one-dish meal. I usually serve it with stewed fruit and hot honey bread.

FINNAN HADDIE
(SERVES SIX)

One of my forebears in the early West was a Scotswoman who wore immaculate white aprons and smoked a tiny pipe. She called eggs "yeggs" and spoke with a thick accent. She was a wee wisp of a thing who carried buckets too big for her frail strength to water her struggling orchard, and bore eight children to build her part of the West. She saw one of them become a governor's wife and the other seven settle on seven sprawling ranches before she got to rest, and her daily lunch was tea served with black bread and cheese. If the smoked cod that is the basis for FINNAN HADDIE had been available those hundreds of miles from the coast, she would have reveled in that traditional Scots dish.

2 or 3	*smoked finnan haddie fillets*
1 to 1½	*cups cream or evaporated milk*
6 to 8	*teaspoons butter or margarine*

Place fillets in a baking dish with their sides just touching. Pour cream or evaporated milk to reach the tops of the fish, and dot with butter or margarine. Bake in a 350° F. oven 45 minutes.

FINNAN HADDIE is traditionally served with boiled potatoes, and I like to add a fruit salad.

TUNA ROLL
(SERVES FOUR TO SIX)

I am including this recipe because it is good, quick, inexpensive, and when my tall son was small he loved it.

2   *cups biscuit mix and enough milk to make a soft dough—about* ⅔ *cup*

2   *6½-oz. cans tuna*

1   *medium onion, peeled and finely chopped*

½   *cup finely chopped celery*

1   *egg, slightly beaten*

1   *cup cheese sauce or 1 10 ¾-oz. can cream of celery soup*

Stir together biscuit mix and milk to make a soft dough. Knead a half dozen times and roll out into a 14″ × 9″ rectangle. Drain tuna and mix with onion, celery, and egg. Spread mixture over biscuit dough, roll up like a jelly roll, and seal ends together. Place on a well-greased cookie sheet, edge side down. Slash at 5 even intervals. Bake at 350° F. for 25 minutes.

Serve with sauce or heated soup, undiluted, dribbled over. When our son, Mark, was a little boy, he thought it was best when served with jello salad and bread sticks.

TWO ITALIAN SEA SONGS

Fisherman's Wharf is one of the most colorful parts of San Francisco. Fishing boats rub against wharf pilings and mingle their creak with the mournful cries of circling seagulls; the briny smell of the sea blends with steam rising from huge pots of boiling shrimp and crab; fog horns groan in counterpoint to a far-off clang of cable cars.

In misty dawns the fishing fleet slips off to sea, manned through generations by Italian fishermen, with crisp hair and dancing eyes. When I am a creaking eighty, my dependable mind's eye will call back the whole scene with all its tastes and smells and sounds, and my taste buds will demand one more plate of broiled shrimp and one more bowl of choppiano.

BROILED SHRIMP ITALIAN STYLE

(SHOULD SERVE EIGHT, BUT YOU'LL EAT SO
MUCH THAT YOU'D BETTER COUNT ON JUST SIX)

Shrimp is so expensive that the only way you can ever justify this recipe is if you are pretty sure you will perish unless you indulge yourself with a plateful.

2	*pounds jumbo shrimp*
½	*cup flour*
¼	*cup cooking or olive oil*
1½	*cups melted butter or margarine*
2	*teaspoons finely minced garlic*
2	*tablespoons finely minced parsley*

Shell shrimp, leaving tails on. Dust lightly with flour. Stir oil and ½ cup melted butter together, and spread in a flat baking dish. Place shrimp in dish and broil at medium heat for 8 minutes. Add garlic and parsley to 1 cup melted butter and pour over shrimp. Stir until shrimp are coated, and broil 2 or 3 minutes longer.

Serve with a green salad tossed with an oil and vinegar dressing, hot buttered rice, and slices of warm french bread with garlic butter.

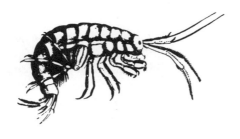

CHOPPIANO

(A LOT DEPENDS ON WHAT VORACIOUS APPETITES YOUR GUESTS HAVE.)

This dish is similar to bouillabaisse, but I think it is even better. It is a traditional Italian dish, and regardless of how it is spelled, in our part of the country it is pronounced "sha-PING." Serve it in big bowls, and it is hospitable to tie towels around guests' necks to protect them from slops and drips. Eat with gusto. Dunk your bread in the sauce. Lick your fingers. Wipe your chin on your neck-towel. Vote for environmental protection bills that will insure a good catch from the sea for the brave little boats.

2	onions, peeled and chopped
1	garlic clove, sliced very thinly
4	stalks celery, sliced
½	cup olive or cooking oil
1	#2½ can tomatoes, mashed
1	quart tomato juice
	juice of 1 lemon
1	bay leaf
	salt and pepper
¼	teaspoon oregano
¼	teaspoon basil
½	teaspoon rosemary
3	pounds fish—red snapper, flounder, sole, haddock, or a combination of two or more—cut into 2-inch squares
1	dozen clams, in the shell
1	dozen jumbo shrimp, in the shell
6	crab legs, in the shell, plus crab meat pulled from the body

Sauté onion, garlic, and celery in oil until golden. Pour into a very large soup kettle. Add tomatoes, tomato juice, lemon juice, and bay leaf. Simmer 20 minutes. Scrub shellfish very well, add to the sauce, and stir in seasonings. Simmer 10 minutes. Add fish and simmer 10 minutes. Add 1 cup white wine, if desired, and simmer an additional 5 minutes.

Ladle into serving bowls, getting a variety of seafood in each bowl with ample amounts of the broth. Serve with big crusty wedges of french bread or hard rolls—for sopping in the sauce.

For a delicious variation, substitute a quart of shucked oysters for the fish—or add them to it.

CAUTION: COSTLY

These two recipes are so expensive that only an unworried budget could afford them. However, if you are ever in a mood (or condition!) to throw caution to the winds—or if a truly memorable occasion needs celebrating—consider one of these:

SHRIMP CREOLE
(SERVES SIX TO EIGHT)

¼ cup butter
1 bunch green onions, finely chopped
4 stalks celery, diced
1 green pepper, chopped
2 #2½ cans tomatoes, mashed
1 cup tomato juice
12 fresh mushrooms, sliced
2 bay leaves
¼ teaspoon thyme
  dash tabasco sauce
  salt and pepper
3 pounds fresh shrimp, cleaned and deveined

Sauté onions, celery, and green pepper in butter. Add remaining ingredients except shrimp. Simmer gently 1 hour. If sauce is too thick, add additional tomato juice. Add shrimp and cook over low heat 10 minutes. Serve over rice.

SEA-SPELL CASSEROLE

(SERVES SIX TO EIGHT)

4 *5-oz. cans deveined shrimp*
4 *6½-oz. cans crab meat*
3 *cups shredded stale bread*
1 *cup finely chopped peeled onion*
1 *cup minced celery*
2 *tablespoons capers*
2 *tablespoons lemon juice*
1 *tablespoon minced parsley*
1 *tablespoon Worcestershire sauce*
1 *tablespoon caper liquid*
2 *teaspoons dry mustard*
½ *teaspoon curry powder*
1 *cup mayonnaise*

Drain shrimp, reserving liquid. Mix all ingredients together with 1 cup shrimp liquid. Bake in a 3-quart casserole at 350° F. for 1 hour. Add additional liquid, if necessary.

Serve with a light salad, dinner rolls, and cheese for dessert.

FISH SAUCES

Fish is so delicately flavored that many people prefer it served with a sauce to perk the flavor. These are our favorites:

DEVIL BUTTER

Combine 6 tablespoons softened butter or margarine with 3 tablespoons softened bleu cheese and 1 tablespoon anchovy paste. Dissolve ½ teaspoon dry mustard in 1 teaspoon white vinegar and 1 teaspoon lemon juice. Blend into butter mixture. Serve at room temperature.

CUCUMBER SAUCE

Combine ¾ cup sour cream with ¼ teaspoon prepared mustard, ½ teaspoon salt, 1 teaspoon grated onion, ¼ teaspoon minced parsley, ½ cup chopped cucumber, and juice of ½ lemon. Chill.

SCOTCH SAUCE

Combine ⅓ cup melted butter or margarine with juice of ½ lemon and ⅓ cup drained capers. Serve warm.

FRISCO SAUCE

Mix 1 cup mayonnaise with ¼ cup ketchup, 1 teaspoon horseradish, 1 teaspoon Worcestershire sauce, salt, pepper, 2 tablespoons grated onion, and 1 tablespoon minced celery. Chill.

WHARF SAUCE

Combine ½ cup chili sauce with ⅓ cup ketchup, ¼ cup horseradish, 1½ teaspoons Worcestershire sauce, ¼ teaspoon salt, 2 tablespoons lemon juice, dash pepper, and ¼ cup minced celery. Chill.

FINNY FILLING FOR SANDWICHES

Leftover fish can happen, and when it does—and you have as much as a cup of it—try this for those sandwiches you are always making.

    1   *cup leftover fish, with skin and bones carefully removed*
    3   *tablespoons finely minced celery*
    2   *tablespoons finely minced peeled onion*
    ½   *teaspoon salt*
         dash pepper
    1   *or 2 small sweet pickles, chopped finely*
    ½   *cup mayonnaise, about*

Mash fish and blend in remaining ingredients. Use enough mayonnaise to make the mixture spread easily.

Chapter 6

BEANS INSTEAD OF MEAT

In the Old West, a girl grew up simply knowing how to cook beans. This chapter is for those who need a little help.

There are many more recipes for beans than there are varieties of beans, but a lot of them aren't worth the effort. There are a few easy tricks to remember about beans, no matter what kind you are cooking. First, they must be washed in cold running water. It's easiest to do this in a colander, letting the beans run slowly through your fingers into the colander so that you can remove any bits of dirt or gravel that may have slipped past the packager. Then run cold water through them to rinse them clean.

The second trick, if it may be called that, is to put the beans to soak overnight in cold water to cover. In the morning, remove any "floaters." According to backcountry lore, the "floaters" are gassy, and removing them will make the final results more sufferable—or less insufferable, depending on your point of view. When you start your bean pot in the morning, start the beans in the same water they have soaked in overnight.

If you forget to put the beans to soak the night before, all is not lost. In the morning, wash the beans, cover them with cold water, and bring them quickly to a boil. Turn off the heat and let them sit for a few minutes. Some floaters will rise to the surface of the water. Remove them. Proceed as if you had soaked them overnight.

The third trick is to refrain from adding too much water at one time while the beans are cooking. Keep the water level 1 to 2 inches over the top of the beans. Add water boiling from the teakettle as soon as the water level drops to less than an inch over the top of the beans. This is what makes them mealy all the way through. Never add cold water to the cooking beans, as it will make them tough.

The last trick is for purists. If you are foresighted and want truly superior beans, cook them, let them stand overnight, and reheat slowly before serving them the following day.

Beans are a good source of protein, as well as phosphorous, iron, and calcium; but in order to supply an adequate protein source, beans should be served with animal protein such as meat, cheese, milk, or eggs. The resulting set of proteins is of higher biological value than either the vegetable protein or the meat protein served alone.

That's the end of the lecture on the care and feeding of a pot of beans. The only thing left to do is to decide which bean recipe you want to try— a spicy ranch style, swimming in a rich gravy with meat; plain beans with ham in an honest broth; beans flavored with garlic and beer; or beans seasoned sweet with molasses and brown sugar.

RANCH BEANS
(SERVES SIX—WITH LEFTOVERS)

These are true Western beans, bred in the Southwest and touched by the Northwest, hearty and filling. My family likes them best served with biscuits, and peaches sliced in cream for dessert.

1   *2-pound package pinto beans*
6   *whole chili tepines*
1   *large onion, peeled and chopped*
1   *#303 can tomatoes, mashed*
1   *8-oz. can tomato sauce*
1   *clove garlic, crushed*
1   *bay leaf*
1   *pound hamburger*

Wash and pick over beans, then put to soak overnight in cold water to cover generously or use the quick-soak method in the morning. Remove any floaters. If you ordinarily have dinner at 6 P.M., start the beans simmering very slowly at about 9 in the morning. Add boiling water as needed to keep the water level about an inch over the beans. After 4 hours, add the tepines (crush them between your fingers as you add them to the pot), onions, tomatoes, tomato sauce, garlic, and bay leaf. Sauté the hamburger lightly, stirring to break it up, and add it to the beans with the pan juices. Continue at a very slow simmer until done—3 or 4 hours longer. Keep the lid on during cooking, and add salt to taste just before serving.

A word of caution about those tepines: They are very small, dried chilies, round in shape and tan in color, and they are *hot.* Crush them into the pot of beans if you like spicy foods, and increase or decrease the quantity to suit your own taste. Whatever you do, *do not* touch your eyes with fingers that have touched chili tepines until you have washed your hands as thoroughly as if you were going to perform surgery. The oil from the tepines clings to your fingers and will burn unmercifully if it gets into your eyes.

IDAHO BEANS
(SERVES SIX HEARTILY)

My grandmother, a ranchwoman who was born in the sagebrush country of Idaho, cooked beans this way and served them to the ranch hands at roundup —probably one reason my grandfather, a French-Indian of wit and pride, never had any trouble hiring help.

1   *2-pound package pink or pinto beans*
1   *#303 can tomatoes, mashed*
1   *large onion, peeled and chopped*
4   *ham hocks or 1 meaty ham bone with trimmings*

Wash and pick over beans, then soak overnight in cold water to cover generously or use the quick-soak method in the morning. Remove any floaters. Bring to a slow simmer. Add all remaining ingredients and simmer slowly all day. Add boiling water as needed to keep the water level an inch over the beans. Remove from heat in the evening and let set, covered, overnight. Just before serving, season to taste with salt and pepper, and heat until hot through. (Since the bean broth is so delicious, you may want to keep the water level at 2 or 3 inches over the beans.)

Serve with rye bread and fruit salad.

MORTAL BEANS

(SERVES FOUR GENEROUSLY)

In the Lost River country of southeast Idaho, a man who had taken a wee nip too much of the bottle and let his whiskey show was said to be "mortal." To this day, I can hear my grandmother's disapproving voice saying, "My, he's mortal, isn't he!" when a cowhand (probably a relative) lurched out of the saloon door. These beans may be "mortal" in beer, but they are immortal in taste. (By the way, heating quickly evaporates the alcoholic content of beer and wine used in cooking, leaving only the flavors.)

1   *1-pound package pinto or kidney beans*
2   *ham hocks or one 4" × 4" piece of salt pork*
1   *bud garlic, crushed*
2   *tablespoons cooking fat*
1   *green pepper, chopped*
2   *ripe tomatoes, chopped*
1   *onion, peeled and chopped*
2   *stalks celery, chopped*
    salt and pepper to taste
1   *can beer*

Wash and pick over beans, then soak overnight in cold water to cover generously or use the quick-soak method in the morning. Remove any floaters. Add ham hocks or salt pork, and garlic; and simmer, keeping the beans constant with an inch of water over them. When the beans are tender —after about 6 hours—drain and reserve liquid. Heat 2 tablespoons fat in a large skillet and sauté green pepper, tomato, onion, and celery until soft, stirring frequently. Stir in drained beans and simmer 10 minutes, stirring often. Add bean liquid, and salt and pepper to taste. Simmer 20 minutes. Stir in beer, heat briefly, and serve with a pan of corn bread and a greens salad.

STANLEY BASIN BEANS
(SERVES SIX TO EIGHT)

The Stanley Basin of Idaho is unforgettably beautiful. It spreads roughly between Galena Pass to the south and Challis to the north in the central part of the state. It is a big, high valley surrounded by the fabled Sawtooth Mountains. The jagged peaks soar wild and fierce above the valley, and the Salmon River, newly born, meanders through grassy bottomland. It is sheep and beef country, but there are also antelope, deer, elk, and bighorn sheep. The weather can be savage. Winter can lay ten feet of snow in the basin, the temperature can drop to sixty degrees below zero, and the winds can rage and tear around the few buildings and two dirt streets that make up the town of Stanley.

There are really two towns of Stanley—Upper Stanley and Lower Stanley. A Stanley native once told me that a fire long ago destroyed most of what is now called Upper Stanley. Some of the residents relocated down-river a mile and called the new settlement Lower Stanley, while the rest of the citizenry remained in the old town to rebuild it.

A few people stay in town during the winter, but only enough to say the town is alive. They need sturdy fare to weather the weather, and STANLEY BASIN BEANS fill the bill.

2　*pounds dried small navy beans*
1　*meaty ham bone with trimmings*
1　*large onion, peeled and chopped*
2　*stalks celery, chopped*
1　*teaspoon pepper*
1　*bay leaf*
　　salt to taste

Wash and pick over beans, then soak overnight in water to cover generously or use the quick-soak method in the morning. Remove any floaters. Add ham bone and trimmings. Keep the water level about 2 inches over these beans so there will be ample broth. Cover and bring to a slow simmer. Continue simmering until the beans start to get tender—about 6 hours—then add remaining ingredients and continue to simmer another 2 hours. When the beans are done, remove ham bone and pull off remaining meat. Shred meat and return to beans. Adjust seasonings to taste.

Serve with hot rolls, and gingerbread for dessert.

VINEGAR BEANS

(SERVES FOUR TO SIX)

The original recipe for these beans drifted west with early settlers, from sod shanties on the Kansas prairie to log cabins in western mountains. Adapted to modern cooking, VINEGAR BEANS are still filling and savory. Be gentle with that vinegar.

1 *pound small navy or pea beans*
¼ *pound salt pork, diced*
1 *large onion, peeled and diced*
2 *cups beef bouillon*
1 *bay leaf*
¼ *cup cider vinegar*

Wash and pick over beans, then soak overnight in cold water to cover generously or use the quick-soak method in the morning. Remove any floaters. Simmer 3 hours, keeping water level 2 inches over top of beans. Fry salt pork over medium heat until crisp. Add onions to salt pork and sauté until onions are transparent, stirring frequently so onions do not brown. Add salt pork, onions, and remaining ingredients to beans. Simmer slowly until beans are done—about 2 hours. Salt and pepper to taste.

Serve with biscuits, and cottage cheese and pear salad.

HAM 'N BEANS

(SERVES EIGHT)

For the sake of variety, try HAM 'N BEANS with pinto beans instead of white beans. The taste is rich and different. My family has feasted on beans cooked this way over a driftwood fire on the wild and lonely northern California coast, with cold corn bread and currant jelly for a taste accompaniment and the crash of surf on rock to listen to.

> 1   *2-pound package pinto beans*
> 1   *ham bone with trimmings*
> 1   *onion, peeled and chopped*
> ¼   *teaspoon basil*
>   *pinch oregano*
> ¼   *teaspoon garlic powder*
>   *salt and pepper to taste*

Wash and pick over beans, then soak overnight in cold water to cover generously or use the quick-soak method in the morning. Remove floaters. Submerge bone and trimmings in the beans. Add water to 1 inch over top of beans. Add remaining ingredients. Simmer gently until done—about 6 hours—adding boiling water as needed to keep water level constant. Adjust seasonings as needed before serving.

Coleslaw is good with these beans, as are hard rolls warmed and spread with herb butter.

HOT-POT BEANS
(SERVES FOUR)

If beans are a major part of your family menu, whether by inclination or by the dictates of income, one of the easiest ways to vary the taste appeal of a dish that might otherwise become tiresome is to vary the meat used in the recipe. Ham or ham hocks instead of hamburger changes the flavor of a traditional bean recipe built around ground meat. This recipe, adapted from a dish served at a hole-in-the-wall restaurant in San Francisco, is a new variety on the old theme.

By the way, the "gut" of salami referred to in the following recipe is a length of dry salami traditionally served as a snack or in sandwiches. They once were encased in a length of animal intestine—hence the old term.

  1   *1-pound package kidney, pink, or pinto beans*
  1   *large onion, peeled and chopped*
  2   *stalks celery, sliced*
 ¼ *cup butter or margarine*
     salt and pepper
  1   *"gut" Italian-style or German dry salami, 14 ounces to 1 pound in weight, cut into bite-sized chunks*

Wash and pick over beans, then soak overnight in cold water to cover generously or use the quick-soak method in the morning. Remove any floaters. Bring quickly to a simmer, cover, reduce heat, and simmer gently until beans are tender—about 6 hours. Keep water level about 1 inch over beans. Cook onion and celery in butter until soft, stirring frequently. Add this mixture, seasonings and salami chunks to beans and simmer 20 minutes.

Serve with sliced tomatoes or cucumber salad, with pumpernickel bread on the side.

FARM BEANS
(SERVES FOUR)

These beans are a candidate for a family favorite—rich, spicy, and filling. They are as nutritious as they are filling, and you need serve with them only bread for dunking in the rich broth. We like hard rolls dunked in ours, and have taken a pot of these savory beans with us on snowshoe or ski trips to reheat over a camp stove.

1	1-pound package pinto beans
1	large onion, peeled and chopped
2	cloves garlic, mashed
1	bay leaf
½	pound ham, bacon, or salt pork, cubed
	salt and pepper
1	#303 can tomatoes, mashed
1	green pepper, chopped
2	teaspoons chili powder
2	tablespoons brown sugar
½	teaspoon dry mustard
¼	teaspoon rosemary

Wash and pick over beans, then soak overnight in cold water to cover generously or use the quick-soak method in the morning. Remove any floaters. Simmer with onion, garlic, and bay leaf for 4 hours, keeping water level 1 inch over top of beans. Add remaining ingredients. Cover tightly and bake in a 350 ° F. oven until done—about 2 hours. Watch the water level carefully and keep it over the beans by about 1 inch.

TILLIE'S BEANS

(SERVES FOUR TO SIX)

Baked beans are basically a New England specialty and are not a native Western dish. However, they are good and everyone should know what they are all about. I found a good recipe for baked beans written in a prim script on a fragile piece of paper folded in an old German song book that I bought for fifty cents at a bookstall in San Francisco. The paper had the recipe on one side, and on the other a letter dated June 11, 1898, from Baltimore, written to "Dear Tillie." I don't know anything about Tillie, but Tillie knew something about beans.

4	cups small white beans
1	6″ × 8″ piece salt pork
¼	cup white sugar
½	cup brown sugar
1	cup molasses
1	large onion, peeled and chopped
1	tablespoon dry mustard
½	cup ketchup

Wash and pick over beans, then soak overnight in cold water to cover generously or use the quick-soak method in the morning. Remove any floaters. Cook at a medium simmer until the skins shrivel when you blow on them—about 1½ hours. Turn the beans into a bean pot or heavy kettle with a tightly fitting lid. Slash the salt pork every inch and press it into the beans. Add sugars, molasses, onion, mustard, and ketchup. Add boiling water to cover. (There should be at least 1 inch of space between the top of the beans and the lid.) Cover tightly and bake in a slow oven (250° to 300° F.) for about 6 hours, checking every half hour and adding boiling water whenever the water level drops below the top of the beans. Uncover during the last half hour to brown. It takes a full day of bean-sitting to get a proper "do" on them, but the results are worth the effort. Vary the quantities of sugar to suit your own sweet taste.

Go traditional all the way and serve TILLIE'S BEANS with corn bread and a plate of juicy pickles, or Boston-style with brown bread and fish cakes.

BAKED BEANS WITH HAM

(SERVES FOUR TO SIX)

This recipe for baked beans is spicier than Tillie's, and is included for the sake of variety.

Serve these beans with coleslaw, and with an "apple-y" dessert such as apple roll or baked apples.

1	1-pound package pea beans or Great Northerns
1	onion, peeled and chopped
⅓	cup ketchup
⅓	cup molasses
1	tablespoon vinegar
¼	teaspoon tabasco sauce
1	teaspoon dry mustard
1	smoked ham shank, about 3 pounds, or a leftover bone with meaty scraps from a ham or pork shoulder roast

Wash and pick over beans, then soak overnight in cold water to cover generously or use the quick-soak method in the morning. Remove any floaters. Add onion, and cook until beans are tender—about 4 hours. Drain, saving 2 cups liquid. Mix liquid with ketchup, molasses, vinegar, tabasco, and mustard. Put ham shank or bone in a large kettle with a tightly fitting lid. Pour beans around shank or bone, and pour liquid over all. Cover and bake at 300° F. for 1½ hours. Remove ham shank or bone, and put bean pot back in oven. Bake, uncovered, for 1 hour—adding boiling water if needed to keep top of beans moist. Shred meat from shank or bone and add to beans. Bake 30 minutes longer.

BEEF 'N BEANS

(SERVES FOUR)

BEEF 'N BEANS is just as good a taste-marriage as HAM 'N BEANS, or bread 'n jelly, or salt 'n pepper. I got this recipe from a friend who, although I love her dearly, is the worst cook I know. Perhaps that isn't a very positive recommendation for the beans, but this is the only thing she can cook that is good—and it is very, very good.

She always serves these beans—and so do I—with garlic french bread cut into chunks, and elegant strawberry ice cream sundaes for dessert.

1	1-pound package pea beans
1	pound hamburger, or 1 pound round steak cut into cubes
1	green pepper, diced
1	onion, peeled and diced
2	stalks celery, diced
1	cup tomato juice
1	8-oz. can tomato sauce
1	tablespoon ketchup
½	cup water
2	tablespoons vinegar
1	teaspoon dry mustard
½	teaspoon thyme
1	tablespoon brown sugar

Wash and pick over beans, then soak overnight in cold water to cover generously or use the quick-soak method in the morning. Remove any floaters. Bring to a simmer and cook until beans are tender—4 to 5 hours. Drain. Lightly sauté meat with green pepper, onion, and celery. Add with all remaining ingredients to beans and stir gently until blended. Place in baking dish and bake at 375° F. for 45 minutes. During the cooking, keep water level 1 inch over top of beans. During the last 45 minutes, add extra tomato juice to moisten if beans get too dry.

COMPANY BEANS
(SERVES SIX TO EIGHT)

A big bowl of fragrant beans cooked especially for the occasion, served with a crisp salad and light rolls, shared with good friends sprawled in front of a fire with light glowing from old kerosene lamps, creates a feeling very close to love.

1	*1-pound package pinto beans*
1	*onion, peeled and chopped*
1	*bay leaf*
1	*clove garlic, mashed*
3	*tablespoons cooking oil*
2	*pounds hamburger*
1	*quart tomato juice*
4	*tablespoons chili powder*
1½	*teaspoon cumin*
¼	*teaspoon pepper*
	salt to taste

Wash and pick over beans, then soak overnight in cold water to cover generously or use the quick-soak method in the morning. Remove any floaters. Add onion, bay leaf, garlic, and cooking oil. Bring rapidly to a boil, reduce heat to a simmer, cover tightly, and simmer 2 hours. Remove bay leaf. Brown meat lightly and add to beans. Remove ⅓ cup of the bean liquid to a small bowl and mix to a smooth paste with the chili powder and cumin. Add to beans along with tomato juice, and stir well. Salt to taste, and add pepper. Bring to a boil, reduce heat, cover tightly, and simmer 2 hours.

OLD-FASHIONED CHILI BEANS
(SERVES FOUR TO SIX)

In the Southwest, it is considered dangerously close to a sin to mention chili in the same breath with beans. There, chili is chili and beans are beans, and never are the two mixed—or rarely, anyway. In the Northwest, we like 'em blended. That is how my grandmother made chili beans. She served them with homemade bread and broiled peaches.

2	pounds hamburger
1	#2½ can tomatoes, mashed
1	can tomato soup, undiluted
3½	cups cooked pink or pinto beans
1	large onion, peeled and chopped
1	teaspoon pepper
2	tablespoons chili powder
½	teaspoon cayenne pepper
¼	teaspoon basil
	salt to taste

Crumble meat as finely as possible and braise slightly. Place in large kettle and add all ingredients. Add hot water to 1 inch over top of mixture. Simmer, covered, 1 hour.

CHILI CON CARNE
(SERVES SIX)

Sometimes, during the long, companionable days of summer, we like to spend a day just gypsying—piling into the car with the inevitable cameras and notebooks, but with no destination in mind. We always take food for the entire day, planning on dinner wherever we happen to be, and just start out. Impulse dictates roads to take and turnings to make. We've never made it more than thirty miles from home before somebody started breaking into the picnic basket to nibble on something. Why we aren't fat, every one of the four of us, I don't know.

One day turned out to be particularly special in our memories. We wandered over miles of dirt roads, seeing not one other person the entire day, and found ourselves at day's end in a Montana ghost town. We strolled through the pioneer cemetery, reading faded inscriptions on weathered wooden headboards, and ambled through what was left of the town, investigating shells of stores and homes and speculating about who lived there and what happened here. Boards flapped and ground squirrels scolded us, and the evening breeze smelled of sage. We had brought along a pot of these beans, and we made coffee to go with them from water we drew out of the town's old, stone-walled spring. Sunset and evening shadows flowed across hills and valley, and meadowlarks sang a song of liquid gold.

1	*cup dried pinto beans*
3	*pounds lean round steak*
¼	*cup cooking oil*
1	*bay leaf*
1	*tablespoon chili powder*
4	*cloves garlic, crushed*
1	*teaspoon cruched cumin seeds*
1	*teaspoon oregano*
1	*tablespoon salt*
2	*tablespoons paprika*
3	*tablespoons cornmeal*
1	*tablespoon flour*

Wash and pick over beans, then soak overnight in cold water to cover generously or use the quick-soak method in the morning. Remove any floaters. Simmer beans 4 hours in water to cover. Drain, reserving liquid. Cut meat into bite-sized cubes, and sear in hot oil. Add to beans. Measure liquid and hot water, if needed, to make 6 cups. Add to beans. Cover, bring to a boil, lower heat, and simmer 1 hour. Add seasonings and simmer ½ hour. Blend cornmeal, flour, and enough water to make a paste. Stir into bean mixture and simmer 5 minutes.

Chapter 7

POTATOES AND OTHER FILLERS

White people usually think the history of this country started when the first white men discovered the continent. It's a shortsighted conclusion, considering that many civilizations of Indians had been developing on the continent for thousands of years before Columbus arrived.

Indians did well with the land. Almost half the crops grown in today's total world food supply were first grown by American Indians, including potatoes.

What we would do without potatoes to help satisfy hunger I don't know. Potatoes are good-tasting, filling, easy to prepare, and inexpensive; contain important food values; and may be prepared many different ways.

BAKED POTATOES

To bake potatoes, start by cleaning them well in warm water so the skins may be eaten after baking. With a dab of butter and a dash of salt they are delicious—and most of the food value is in the skins.

I always cut a narrow slice off both ends of each potato before I bake it. My sister-in-law once asked me why I did it, and I was dumbfounded to discover I didn't know why. My mother sliced off spud ends and so did my grandmother, and I followed along unquestioningly. I finally learned that I slice the ends to prevent the potatoes from exploding in the oven.

Before baking, grease potatoes with bacon drippings, lard, shortening, butter, or margarine; put them either in a baking pan or directly on the oven rack and bake in a moderate (350° F.) oven until they are soft all the way through—about an hour for average-sized potatoes. Serve them with butter, salt, and a sprinkle of freshly ground pepper, or with a bowl of chilled sour cream.

Baking is a good way to prepare potatoes as the nutritional value is high, there is no preparation expense or effort to speak of, and they are desirable as leftovers to make into breakfast hashbrowns, to turn into potato salad, or to slice into a skillet for fried potatoes.

If baked potatoes have to wait before serving, wrap them together snugly in a clean, heavy bath towel. They will stay warm without getting hard.

Baked potatoes are adaptable, so occasionally vary your menus with one of the following ideas:

BAKED BACON

Wrap each potato in a slice of bacon, skewer the ends of the bacon to the potato with toothpicks, and wrap in individual foil blankets. Bake as usual. Push the foil down the last 20 minutes so the bacon will crisp.

CREAM BAKED

Bake 2 large potatoes until done. Cool slightly. Cut into halves and carefully scoop out centers, being careful not to tear the shells. Whip potatoes with 2 tablespoons melted butter or margarine mixed with ¼ cup hot milk. Blend in ¼ cup heavy cream or evaporated milk, and season to taste with salt and pepper. Refill shells and brush tops of potato with egg white. Place in buttered baking dish and bake in a hot (400° F.) oven 10 minutes. Serves four.

CHEESE BAKED

Follow recipe for CREAM BAKED and add ⅓ cup grated cheese to potato mixture.

HAM BAKED

Follow recipe for CREAM BAKED and add ½ cup chopped cooked ham to potato mixture.

GERMAN BAKED

Follow recipe for CREAM BAKED and add to potato mixture ¼ cup finely chopped green onion, 2 slices bacon, diced and cooked until crisp, and 1 finely chopped dill pickle.

SPANISH BAKED

Follow recipe for CREAM BAKED and add 2 tablespoons finely chopped onion, 2 tablespoons finely chopped green pepper, and ¼ cup finely chopped tomato. Top with a sprinkle of shredded cheddar or American cheese before serving.

DEALER'S CHOICE BAKED

Follow recipe for CREAM BAKED and add 1 cup of cooked sausage, crumbled, or ½ cup thinly sliced frankfurter.

MASHED POTATOES

A bowl piled to the brim with snowy mashed potatoes is hard to resist; and before you think they are too fattening, please remember that a potato has only as many calories as an apple. Help yourself. It is what you add to them that you must watch.

Mashed potatoes should be light and creamy. Start by figuring 1 large spud for each person, and add an extra potato for every third person—that makes 5 spuds for four people. Pare and cut in chunks. Put in salted cold water, bring to a boil rapidly, and continue boiling until potatoes are completely done—about 25 minutes.

When you pare potatoes and are not going to cook them immediately, put them in cold water to cover to keep them from turning dark—but don't let them set too long or they will be sticky. A bit of vinegar in the cooking water is supposed to lighten potatoes that have turned dark while waiting to cook. Potatoes with a greenish cast to them have been sunburned and are apt to be bitter.

As soon as the potatoes have finished boiling, drain well immediately and reserve cooking liquid. Mash potatoes roughly. In a small saucepan heat milk, potato water, and butter, figuring ¼ cup milk, ¼ cup potato water, and 2 tablespoons butter or margarine for every 4 potatoes. Pour the hot milk mixture over the potatoes and stir while pouring, then whip hard— an electric mixer helps. Season with salt and pepper to taste, pile into a bowl, and top with a generous glob of butter. For variety, try one of the following:

SIERRA STYLE

Whip 5 large boiled potatoes and keep them hot. Whip ½ cup heavy cream until stiff. Fold in ¼ cup shredded cheddar or American cheese. Fold cream mixture into potatoes and pile gently into a baking dish. Pop into a 400° F. oven about 10 minutes or until delicately browned.

CASCADE STYLE

Whip 5 large boiled potatoes and keep hot. Stir 2 slices bacon, fried crisp and crumbled, into ½ cup heavy cream. Pile whipped potatoes into a baking dish and pour cream mixture over top. Sprinkle with ½ cup coarse, dried bread crumbs. Bake in a 400° F. oven about 10 minutes or until crumbs have browned.

OLYMPIC STYLE

Whip 5 large boiled potatoes with ¼ teaspoon salt, shake of pepper, ½ cup hot milk, and ½ cup leftover cooked spinach chopped finely.

ROCKIES STYLE

Whip 5 large boiled potatoes with ¼ teaspoon salt, shake of pepper, ½ cup hot milk, and ½ cup thinly sliced celery that has been sautéed in melted butter or margarine until soft.

BOILED POTATOES

Potatoes boiled in their skins are similar to baked potatoes in ease of preparation and nutritional value, and leftovers are used in the same way. Boiled potatoes are the traditional accompaniment to such dishes as FINNAN HADDIE, and are a delicious treatment for red potatoes or new potatoes.

To prepare, select potatoes of uniform size so they will cook evenly, scrub, and cook in boiling water deep enough to cover until tender. They will be done in about 25 minutes.

LOST RIVER STYLE

The Lost River country of Idaho is a land of contrasts and stark beauty. High mountains rise from prairie flats, and lava outcroppings give the landscape an eerie beauty. Sagebrush and sand butts up against meadows of wild hay, and in a hidden ranch in a hidden valley my grandmother cooked potatoes like these. Only red potatoes will do—the Idaho roses.

Boil 5 or 6 red potatoes until tender. Pare. Melt ½ cup butter or margarine in a heavy skillet. Slice potatoes thickly into skillet. Reduce heat and cook slowly until potatoes have a golden crust. Turn carefully and crust the second side. Season with salt and pepper.

FRIED POTATOES

(SERVES FOUR TO SIX)

In the pioneering days of the Old West, one recipe for fried potatoes was known as "Freighter Style" and was justly famous. To cook them, start by frying 4 strips of bacon until golden and crisp in a heavy skillet. Remove bacon and crumble. In the same skillet layer thinly 3 sliced raw potatoes, one thinly sliced peeled onion, and the bacon. Season well with salt and pepper. Pour 1 to 1½ cups hot water over the layers. Cover tightly and cook over low heat until water is absorbed and potatoes are tender—30 to 45 minutes, depending on the type of potatoes and the thickness of the slices. When the bottom of the potato layer has cooked to a golden crust, carefully turn as nearly to all at once as possible, and brown the other side.

For a variation of fried potatoes, slice potatoes thinly and fry in ¼ cup melted bacon drippings in a heavy skillet over a medium heat 30 minutes, turning once. Remove from skillet and keep warm. In the same skillet make 1½ cups thin white sauce and season with ½ teaspoon pepper, 1½ teaspoons salt, and a hearty pinch of ground sage and basil. Add fried potatoes gently and reheat briefly in the sauce.

POLENTA

Instead of potatoes under gravy or sauce, try an Italian-inspired dish called "polenta." I learned about polenta in the old North Beach section of San Francisco. North Beach, the Italian neighborhood of that spun-sugar city by the Golden Gate, has places called bocce ball courts where the citizens play bocce ball, and strolling musicians play and sing for spectators. Some bocce ball courts serve food.

To make polenta, you must have patience.

3   *medium potatoes, peeled and diced finely*
1   *quart water*
2   *teaspoons salt*
¾   *cup yellow cornmeal*

Put potatoes, water, and salt in a deep kettle. Bring to a boil. Add cornmeal *very* slowly, stirring constantly. Simmer over low heat about 45 minutes, stirring all the while. (This is a good time to memorize poetry or finally get the multiplication tables mastered.) When the mixture is stiff, turn onto a buttered platter.

Serve instead of rice, potatoes, or noodles. A spaghetti-type sauce is traditionally spooned over it.

NOODLES

Make your own noodles for a fraction of the cost of store-bought, and for greatly superior flavor. Don't be dismayed at the idea, for making noodles is as easy as falling off a log. You can make a carload at one time and store them in the cupboard in a large jar with a tightly fitting lid.

In a large bowl beat 1 egg slightly. Add enough flour to make a very stiff dough. Knead a few times. Turn onto a slightly floured board and roll paper-thin. This is very important—the noodles will swell as they cook, and if your original product is not very thin you will have gooey noodles. Roll up like a jelly roll. Cut with a very sharp knife into ⅛- or ¼-inch strips. Separate well, shaking them out gently. Dry out on a board for a few hours. When well dried, store in a covered jar until needed. (It is important to use a jar with a threaded lid that will screw on tightly.) For a larger amount of noodles, increase the number of eggs with which you start. Two eggs with enough flour added to make a stiff dough will result in a staggering amount of noodles.

DUMPLINGS

Dumplings may be added to stewed chicken in place of (or in addition to) noodles, on top of any meat-and-gravy casserole, on top of soups to stretch a dinner, over a stew, or cooked on top of broth or gravy.

I make mine by mixing and sifting together 2 cups flour, 4 teaspoons baking powder, and ½ teaspoon salt. Add 1 cup milk gradually, stirring well as you add. Drop by large spoonsful on top of stewed chicken, stew, or what-have-you about 15 minutes before serving. Cover tightly and steam about 12 minutes. Keep tightly covered during cooking and do not peek. The steam in the kettle is what makes the dumplings light; and if, because of your curiosity, the steam escapes before the dumplings are done, the results will be soggy and heavy.

YORKSHIRE PUDDING
(SERVES SIX)

For an under-gravy or under-sauce item, or all by itself with roasts, consider YORKSHIRE PUDDING.

Mix ¼ teaspoon salt with 1 cup flour and add 1 cup milk gradually, stirring to make a smooth paste. Add 2 eggs and beat 2 minutes with an egg beater. Grease an 8″×8″×2″ cake pan or 2 bread pans with a generous amount of fat or butter. Heat the pans. Pour dough mixture about ½-inch deep into the hot pans. Bake in a preheated hot (450° F.) oven for 15 minutes, then reduce heat to 325° F. and bake 15 minutes longer. Cut into squares for serving.

Yorkshire Pudding doesn't stand around waiting very well, so serve immediately.

For such simple ingredients it is uncommonly good, and I don't know why it is called a pudding when it isn't one.

DRESSING

Make a bread dressing to stuff a chicken, a turkey, a fish, or a meatloaf; to put under roasting meat; to wrap inside a flank steak before roasting; to stuff vegetables such as zucchini; or for anything else your imagination comes up with. Call it dressing or stuffing—it's all the same thing.

I've enjoyed chestnut dressing and think oyster dressing is superb. I've made cornbread dressing, sauerkraut dressing, apple dressing, and raisin

dressing. I have experimented with sausage dressings and found each variation very good, but in my mind dressing is sage dressing, the way my grandmother made it in the sweep and space that is Idaho to me.

>   *about 5 cups stale bread, torn into fine pieces, or an equivalent*
>   *amount of prepared stuffing mix*
> 1 *cup peeled and chopped onion*
> 1 *cup chopped celery*
> ¾ *cup butter or margarine*
>   *salt to taste*
> ½ *teaspoon each oregano, marjoram, ground sage, garlic powder*
> ¼ *teaspoon pepper*
>   *hot water*

In a large saucepan put about a quart of water, the chopped onion, celery,
and ¼ cup butter or margarine. Bring to a boil, cover, reduce heat, and
simmer until vegetables are tender—20 to 25 minutes. Strain, reserving
liquid and keeping it hot. Put torn bread in large, flat container in which
you can stir easily, such as a roasting pan. Add drained onion and celery,
and seasonings. Dot with ½ cup butter or margarine. Pour over it the
hot, reserved liquid. Stir thoroughly. The dressing must be very moist at this
stage, so if you do not have enough broth add boiling water or chicken
bouillon, stirring as you add, until the bread mixture is quite moist. Cover
immediately with a clean towel and let mixture steam in its own heat 5
minutes. Taste, and adjust seasonings if necessary. Be cautious with the
ground sage—too little makes a flat dressing, but a trifle too much is
ruinous. (There are various mixed herbs on the market sold as seasonings
specifically for dressings. Some of them are pretty good, if you experiment
until you find proportions you like.) Stir well again, and taste until the flavor
suits you, remembering that the seasonings will increase while the dressing
cooks. Stuff a 12- to 15-pound turkey, or reduce quantities to stuff chicken,
meats or vegetables. Stuff while the dressing is still warm.

When making sage dressing for chicken or turkey, add neck, giblets,
and wing tips, as well as any body fat you can easily pull off, to the simmering celery and onions. Let cool, and mince giblets. Pull meat off neck in
slender shreds. Add to the bread with the celery and onions.

RICE

A stroll through San Francisco's Chinatown is a feast for the senses. Narrow groceries display rows of naked chickens dangling beside goose-pimpled ducks and glazed pigs, and the windows of import firms gleam with gold-thread kimonos and pearls. Incense rides over ginger and smoked fish; tea with jasmine blossoms floating in it is served in paper-thin cups in dim cafés. Jammed streets are noisy with snail-paced traffic and impatient horns, bicycles, paper dragons and shouted Chinese dialects. Moon gates lead into dark alleys; and above the jangling crowds, pagoda roofs and eaves shaped like dragons make a skyline that might as well be in Peiping or Shanghai, Canton or Macau.

The grandsons of Chinese laborers shipped to coastal ports to build mines and railroads now build fine restaurants. Before I grow so old and toothless that I have to sip bland gruel through a straw, I'll go back to Chinatown—in Fresno, Sacramento, Vancouver, Seattle, or San Francisco. I'll savor my way through almond duck and paper chicken, snow peas, bitter melon, egg rolls, butterfly shrimp, and sweet-sour pork, all in one sitting. As a grand finale, I'll finally master the art of eating rice with chopsticks.

No one can cook rice like the Chinese, but Westerners have developed acceptable variations.

Precooked, reconstituted, or prepared rice will not do. White rice is good, but brown rice is better. Buy plain, real, untampered-with rice. Some brands are clean enough to require only a brief cold water rinsing through a sieve. Others need immersion in plentiful quantities of water.

For every cup of rice, bring to a boil 2 to 2½ cups of water. (Experiment to see if you like your rice chewier—the result of less water, or stickier—the result with more water.) When the water is boiling, add ½ teaspoon cooking oil and the rice. Cover tightly, reduce heat, and gently simmer until all the water is taken up—45 minutes to 1 hour. One and one-half cups of rice in 3 cups of water will make dependable servings for four hungry people.

To serve it by itself, in place of potatoes, simply heap the rice in a serving bowl and top with a generous lump of butter or margarine. To make it memorable, pour over the rice spaghetti sauce, gravy, or a sweet-sour sauce that contains chunks of chicken or spareribs.

For a delicious variation, try this version of fried rice:

¼   *cup butter or margarine*
3   *green onions with tops, chopped finely*
1   *stalk celery, chopped finely*
3   *cups cooked rice*
2   *tablespoons soy sauce*

In a large skillet melt butter and add onion and celery. Cook, stirring, until vegetables are tender but still underdone—they will be just transparent. Stir in hot, cooked rice. Add soy sauce, more or less to taste. Stir well to blend.

One of my family's favorite dishes is rice cooked this way, with piping-hot, small whole shrimp blended through the rice just before serving. We like it served with a green salad and hot rolls.

Chapter 8

SALADS AND VEGETABLES— WHEN FRESH FOOD IS HARD TO COME BY

In the days of the Old West, fresh fruits and vegetables were rare treats at best during the long winter months, and an orange was a luxurious Christmas stocking-stuffer for lucky children.

In place of today's year-round supply of lettuce, tomatoes, cucumbers, green peppers, and avocados, salad-hungry pioneers made do with winter-hardy ingredients such as cabbage, apples, celery, nuts, carrots, and canned fruits. The results were delicious.

Scarcity dictated attitudes and solutions to problems that modern families can also find useful. Pioneer treatments of salads and vegetables managed to combine economy with solid nutritional values—and that is a combination which most of today's homemakers are looking for.

NOISY SALAD

(SERVES FOUR)

This salad is actually Waldorf Salad. An everyday salad as it stands, it becomes a holiday treat with the addition of chopped nuts, halved grapes, marshmallow bits, and chopped maraschino cherries.

2   *cups unpeeled diced apple*
1   *cup finely sliced celery*
½   *cup mayonnaise*
2   *tablespoons sugar*

Mix ingredients together. Let stand a few minutes. Stir again gently before serving.

JACKPOT SALAD

(SERVES FOUR)

Everybody in Nevada, where gambling has always been legal, knows what a jackpot is. It's when you feed $10 in nickles into a slot machine and win $7.50—and get excited about it!

SALAD:
1   *cup unpeeled diced apple*
2   *cups finely shredded raw cabbage*

DRESSING:
¾   *cup fruit syrup from a can of peaches or pears*
¼   *cup vinegar*
1   *tablespoon cornstarch*
⅓   *cup sugar*
¼   *teaspoon dry mustard*
1   *tablespoon butter or margarine*

Mix apple and cabbage together. Stir in dressing. Let set for a few minutes, then gently stir again just before serving.

To make the dressing: Mix syrup with vinegar and blend well with cornstarch. Bring to a boil and cook, stirring constantly, about 2 minutes, or until mixture starts to thicken. Blend in sugar, mustard, and butter. Mix well and cool before using.

TANGY SALAD
(SERVES SIX)

SALAD:

1	*cup unpeeled diced apple*
1	*cup pared, finely grated carrot*
3	*cups finely shredded cabbage*

DRESSING:

1	*tablespoon dry mustard*
2	*tablespoons milk*
2	*tablespoons sugar*
2	*tablespoons vinegar*
1/4	*teaspoon salt*

Combine salad ingredients and set aside. In a small mixing bowl, combine dressing ingredients and beat with an egg beater until fluffy. Blend into salad ingredients and chill.

COLESLAW

There can't be more than a hundred different ways to make coleslaw. The following four Western-born recipes for it swell the total—but they are all excellent, inexpensive, and perhaps new to you.

APPLE SLAW
(SERVES SIX)

1   onion, peeled, thinly sliced, and separated into rings
2   unpeeled apples, chopped
4   cups shredded cabbage
⅓   cup finely diced dill pickle
¾   cup of the dressing listed under GREEN SALAD later in this chapter

Combine ingredients and stir gently until all are well mixed.

DUTCHMAN COLESLAW
(SERVES SIX)

4   cups finely shredded cabbage
½   cup sliced green onions
¼   cup finely chopped green pepper
3   tablespoons vinegar
2   tablespoons salad oil
2   tablespoons sugar
1   teaspoon salt

Mix vegetables together. In a small jar with a tightly fitting lid combine remaining ingredients and shake well. Mix into salad mixture and chill before serving.

PRUSSIAN SLAW
(SERVES FOUR)

1   teaspoon salt
1   teaspoon dry mustard
1   teaspoon paprika
1   teaspoon celery seed
½   cup light karo syrup
¼   cup vinegar
1   cup salad oil
3   tablespoons grated peeled onion
3   cups finely shredded cabbage

In a large bowl combine first 7 ingredients and beat until thick. Mix onion with cabbage and fold into dressing mixture.

OLD-FASHIONED COLESLAW
(SERVES SIX TO EIGHT)

The Salmon River flows northward for 175 miles before it turns west to bisect Idaho. From the point of its westward turn, the Salmon has a romantic second name—the "River of No Return"—bestowed in admiration and pride by boatmen who found the wild river navigable downstream but not back up against fierce rapids and falls. (The river's pride has been broken since by roaring jet boats that can quell her spirit.) On the west side of Idaho, the Salmon turns northward again to join the Snake River. The Snake flows into the Columbia, and the Columbia flows to the sea.

On each end of its east-west race across Idaho, the fabled river has a few miles of road for an uneasy companion. The road passes Indian rock shelters that the Sheepeater tribe decorated over five thousand years ago with tally marks and drawings in red dyes, and log cabins that sit on the earth as if they grew there.

The few people who live along the road must drive their children up to sixty miles just to catch the school bus for another twenty-mile ride to classes. In one pretty homesite, with cherry and peach trees on one side and a garden so tidy on the other that weeds wouldn't dare grow there, lives a family whose love for the land is part and parcel of their love for each other. Jean searched for twenty years before she finally found a cole-slaw recipe that pleased Warner. Here it is:

4   *cups thinly shredded cabbage*
1   *small, thinly sliced green pepper*
1   *cup thinly sliced raw cauliflower*
1   *small onion, peeled and chopped finely*
⅓   *cup shredded scraped carrot*
1   *cup granulated sugar*
1   *teaspoon pepper*
    vinegar and water

In a large, deep bowl combine vegetables. Add sugar and pepper. Add vinegar and cold water alternately until the liquid comes up to the top of the cabbage and is tart or sweet enough to suit your taste. Experiment and taste as you add until you have the flavor you like best. Strain the leftover salad to retrieve the dressing, and refrigerate it to use again.

MORMON THREE-BEAN SALAD
(SERVES SIX TO EIGHT)

In hundreds of small towns and some large ones scattered throughout the West, the Mormon Church has divisions called wards and stakes. In each church group, the women have a "Relief Society" which, during the year, holds bazaars—social events of moment for the whole town, Mormon or non-Mormon—where they sell handmade quilts and other handcrafts and put on a dinner that makes my mouth water just to remember: roast turkeys and hams and beef; dressings and gravies; dozens of casseroles; your choice of baked, escalloped, or mashed potatoes, or all three; at least two vegetables; molded salads, potato salads, fruit salads, green salads, and vegetable salads; homemade rolls and bread, with homemade butter, and honey from farm hives; garden pickles and every cook's favorite relishes; a dozen different kinds of pies and cakes; and homemade root beer and ice cream.

The last time my husband and I attended a Relief Society dinner, I pretended I had never seen him before in my life because they had MORMON THREE-BEAN SALAD. He has a fatal weakness for it, and loaded such a huge helping on his smorgasbord plate that his thumb was buried.

1   *#303 can green beans (not french cut)*
1   *#303 can kidney beans*
1   *#303 can either wax or garbanzo beans*
1   *green pepper, sliced*
1   *onion, peeled and thinly sliced*
½   *cup vinegar*
½   *cup salad oil*
¾   *cup sugar*
1   *teaspoon salt*
½   *teaspoon pepper*

Drain beans very well. Place in a bowl with green pepper and onion slices. Combine vinegar with remaining ingredients and mix well. Pour over beans. Stir gently so dressing is well distributed. Refrigerate several hours or overnight. Stir gently again before serving.

STIFF SALAD
(SERVES FOUR)

1   *package lemon or lime gelatin*
2   *cups hot water*
½   *cup shredded cabbage*
2   *tablespoons vinegar*
½   *teaspoon salt*
1   *cup diced unpeeled apple*

Dissolve gelatin in hot water. Chill until slightly thickened. Mix cabbage with vinegar and salt, and let stand 15 minutes. Fold cabbage mixture into apple, and stir both into thickened gelatin. Chill until firm.

ANYTHING SALAD
(SERVES FOUR)

1 *package lime gelatin*
2 *cups hot water*
½ *cup mayonnaise*

ONE OF THE FOLLOWING:
 ½ *cup cottage cheese and ¼ cup well-drained, canned, crushed pineapple;* OR
 1 *cup diced apple;* OR
 ½ *cup diced apple and ½ cup sliced celery;* OR
 ½ *cup marshmallow bits and ½ cup finely shredded cabbage;* OR
 1 *cup leftover cooked vegetables;* OR
 ½ *cup shredded scraped carrot and ½ cup diced apple;* OR
 ½ *cup diced apple and ½ cup halved seedless grapes*

Dissolve gelatin in water and chill until slightly thickened. Add mayonnaise and whip until well mixed. Stir in 1 of the optional ingredients. Chill until firm.

DARK SALAD
(SERVES FOUR TO SIX)

This was my mother's favorite Thanksgiving salad—simple and make-ahead, and a tangy compliment to the richness of holiday dressings and gravies and sauces. It calls for canned fruit because there are no fresh berries in Idaho in November.

1 *large package black raspberry gelatin*
1 *#303 can raspberries, drained (reserve liquid)*
1 *pint sour cream*

Mix gelatin according to package directions, but use ½ cup less water and substitute for it the reserved berry juice. Chill until slightly thickened. Mix in berries and sour cream. Mix thoroughly at slowest speed on electric mixer or vigorously by hand until well whipped. Pour into mold and chill until firm.

MANDARIN SALAD
(SERVES SIX TO EIGHT)

Marin County in California starts at the north end of San Francisco's Golden Gate Bridge. It is a land of hills and woods and charm, with the sea lapping on three sides. Sea-edge towns like Sausalito and Tiburon spawn boats with graceful sails, and forest towns like Mill Valley and Forest Knolls are arranged in settings of redwoods and fern. It is a lovely, gentle place, and I remember MANDARIN SALAD served on a patio blazing with begonias and fuschias and flowering plum.

2 *packages lemon gelatin*
1 *cup hot water*
1 *cup cold water*
1 *6-oz. can frozen orange juice*
2 *buffet cans mandarin oranges, drained (reserve syrup)*
½ *pint whipping cream, whipped*
¾ *cup mayonnaise*
1 *ripe banana, mashed*
⅔ *cup crushed pineapple, drained (reserve syrup)*

Mix gelatin with hot water and stir well. Combine reserved fruit syrups and add cold water, if needed, to make 1 cup. Stir in orange juice. Stir mixture into gelatin. Chill until slightly thickened. Fold in oranges. Chill until set.

Gently but thoroughly blend together whipped cream, mayonnaise, mashed banana, and pineapple. Pour over portions of salad when served. (It is nice to make the salad in a ring mold and unmold onto a platter. Put the dressing in a container inside the hole in the center of the salad so guests may serve themselves.)

TOMATO ASPIC WITH STYLE
(SERVES FOUR TO SIX)

Everybody knows how to make tomato aspic, but all ordinary recipes for it are pallid in comparison to this one, which first delighted me at a taster's luncheon at Lake Tahoe when four feet of snow covered the ground and winter dusk came at four o'clock. Its cheerful color and bright flavor are even more welcome in winter than in summer, when it is usually served.

1   *envelope unflavored gelatin*
2   *cups tomato or tomato-vegetable juice*
1/4 *teaspoon salt*
2   *teaspoons lemon juice*
1   *teaspoon Worcestershire sauce*
1   *vigorous dash of pepper*
1/2 *cup finely chopped celery*
1   *dozen stuffed green olives, sliced*
1   *4½-oz. can shrimp, well drained*

Soften gelatin in juice. Add salt, lemon juice, Worcestershire sauce, and pepper. Stir well. Pour into a mold and chill until slightly thickened. Fold in celery, olives, and shrimp. Chill until set. Unmold onto a pretty plate.

SARDINE SALAD
(SERVES FOUR)

There are pack-in base camps sprinkled throughout the mountains of the West, from five to fifty miles from the nearest road. Some are guide's camps for big game hunters, some are jump-off camps for hikers and backpackers, and ours are "home" for research projects and photo expeditions. A few are luxurious affairs with several sleeping tents, a cook tent, a social tent, cots and chairs and folding bathtubs, and even a portable generator for lights. Some are skimpy, makeshift operations, and most lie somewhere in between the two extremes.

All have one feature in common: The variety of food supplies is limited. It is a hard job to haul supplies by packhorse over steep, switchback trails, and refrigeration is either nonexistent or limited. Salads, consequently, appear only during the early days in camp and thereafter only if someone comes in carrying the ingredients. You wouldn't believe how salad-hungry you can become after a week in camp when you know there isn't any lettuce left.

One time, down to produce supplies consisting of one limp stalk of celery and half a tired head of lettuce, we feasted on a sardine salad created by a short-tempered, old-time camp cook who had forgotten more about trail cookery than most people ever know. (He belonged to the same cantankerous breed as a hunting camp cook named Charlie, who once snorted to an uncomfortable hundred-dollar-a-day dude: "Hunh. Get a thousand dollar rifle and a nine dollar sleeping bag and then bitch about the cold!")

1   *large can sardines (packed in oil), well drained*
4   *hard-cooked eggs, chopped*
¼   *cup finely chopped sweet pickle*
2   *tablespoons finely minced peeled onion*
1   *stalk celery, minced*
½   *cup shredded lettuce*
⅓   *cup mayonnaise*
1   *tablespoon vinegar*
     fruit syrup from canned fruit—3 or 4 tablespoons

Mash sardines with chopped egg. Stir in pickle, onion, and celery. Stir in lettuce. Blend mayonnaise with vinegar, and add fruit syrup until the consistency is thin enough to pour. Pour over salad.

FRUIT SALAD
(SERVES FOUR)

1   *cup diced unpeeled apple*
2   *cups diced peeled oranges*
1   *large banana, thinly sliced*
½   *cup halved seedless grapes*
½   *cup pineapple wedges or peaches cut into chunks*
2   *tablespoons sugar*
⅓   *cup mayonnaise*
    syrup from canned fruit—3 or 4 tablespoons

Combine fruits and sprinkle with sugar. Blend mayonnaise with sufficient syrup from canned fruit to make the mixture fairly thin. Drizzle over fruit and stir gently.

24-HOUR SALAD
(SERVES SIX)

In the close-knit, small towns of the mountain West, communities still respond to an individual's time of crisis.

When there is a death or serious illness in a family, a steady stream of anxious friends and nodding acquaintances beat a path to the door, bearing hot casseroles, cold salads, roasts and potatoes, and cakes—so that the troubled family doesn't have to think about cooking. That often wordless exchange at the door with only a clasp of hands and a look is a moving form of communication, a tangible expression of love and concern and understanding. I remember this old-fashioned salad being delivered at such a doorway meeting.

2   eggs
¼   cup white vinegar
¼   cup sugar
2   tablespoons butter or margarine
1   cup heavy cream, whipped
2   cups quartered marshmallows
1   #303 can pineapple tidbits, drained
1   cup seedless grapes, halved
1   cup drained maraschino cherries, halved
2   oranges, peeled and diced

Beat eggs in top of double boiler. Add vinegar, sugar, and butter; and cook over boiling water, stirring constantly, until thickened. Fold in whipped cream, fruits, and marshmallows. Chill for 24 hours before serving.

CRUNCHY SALAD
(SERVES FOUR)

1   cup thinly sliced raw cauliflower
1   cup thinly sliced peeled onion
½   cup thinly sliced scraped carrot
½   cup dressing listed under GREEN SALAD later in this chapter
      about 2 cups torn crisp lettuce

Combine first 3 ingredients and toss lightly with dressing. Cover and chill 1 hour. When time to serve, add lettuce and toss again. More dressing may be needed, depending on the amount of lettuce you use. To stretch this salad to feed more people, double the quantity of lettuce and keep remaining ingredients the same.

COOL-AS-A-CUCUMBER SALAD
(SERVES FOUR, SKIMPILY)

½ pint sour cream
   generous dash garlic powder
   stingy dash Worcestershire sauce
1 teaspoon lemon juice
5 cucumbers, peeled and chopped
5 green onions, chopped
   salt, pepper, and paprika

Add garlic powder, Worcestershire sauce, and lemon juice to sour cream. In a bowl combine cucumber and onions. Pour sour cream mixture over vegetables and gently stir until well blended. Sprinkle with salt, pepper, and paprika. Chill.

CANARY ISLANDS SALAD
(SERVES FOUR)

If you head west and keep on going far enough and long enough and make all the appropriate transportation changes, sooner or later you will reach the Canary Islands.

A friend of ours did just that (I had to find an atlas to locate the Canary Islands, as I had a vague idea that they were somewhere around Africa or maybe Spain) and came home with this delectable salad that adapts readily to Western foods and palates.

DRESSING:

½ cup salad oil
2 tablespoons lemon juice
½ teaspoon dry mustard
½ teaspoon salt
¼ teaspoon pepper
   pinch rosemary

SALAD:

      approximately 3 cups torn, crisp lettuce
2   *green onions and tops, chopped*
3   *pears, pared and cut into bite-sized chunks*

Combine dressing ingredients in a jar with a tightly fitting lid and shake until very well blended. Combine salad ingredients in a bowl. Pour dressing over salad and toss.

CHRISTMAS SALAD
(SERVES FOUR TO SIX)

In the old days, homesteaders put apples and Christmas pears in fruit cellars and, if it was a good year, bought the golden treasures of oranges as Christmas treats for their children. In this McBride family Christmas dinner salad, the apples and pears of pioneer days are combined with ingredients old-timers probably never heard of.

1   *#303 can pineapple tidbits, drained*
1   *16-oz. jar whole maraschino cherries, drained*
2   *bananas, sliced*
1   *unpared apple, diced*
3   *ripe pears, pared and chopped*
1   *cup chopped walnut meats*
1   *8-oz. container sour cream*

Combine fruits and nut meats in a bowl. Gently stir in sour cream until well blended. Cover with waxed paper and chill.

GREEN SALAD
(SERVES FOUR)

In the Northwest, before the days of refrigerated transportation that made salads available all year-round, the first lettuce and tomatoes of early summer were met with an enthusiasm they have not known since.

A superlative green salad should include several different kinds of greens. A superb combination is iceberg lettuce, romaine, red leaf lettuce, and raw spinach leaves. The greens must be clean and crisp—rinse them very well under cold water and wrap in a towel before refrigerating.

SALAD:

3 *cups assorted greens, torn into bite-sized pieces*
2 *radishes, thinly sliced*
2 *green onions, sliced*
1 *tomato cut into bite-sized pieces*
  about ½ cup green salad dressing (recipe follows)

Tear—do not cut—greens into pieces in a large bowl. Add remaining vegetables. Sprinkle lightly with salt.

DRESSING:

⅔ *cup salad oil*
⅓ *to ½ cup vinegar, depending on your taste*
¼ *teaspoon sugar*
½ *teaspoon salt*
¼ *teaspoon garlic powder*
  pinch each of marjoram, basil, and rosemary
  dash pepper

To make dressing: Combine ingredients in a bottle with a tightly fitting lid. Let stand a few minutes, then shake again. Pour salad dressing over salad and toss until ingredients are well coated. This recipe improves with age, has better flavor than any commercially prepared salad dressing, and costs a fraction as much.

WINTER DOLDRUMS SALAD

(SERVES FOUR)

⅓ *cup honey*
¼ *cup salad oil*
¼ *cup vinegar*
3 *cups of your favorite green salad combination*

I think the best green salad is one of different kinds of crisp, torn greens fresh from the garden, with a ripe tomato cut up over them. Sprinkle with salt and let the salad chill 15 or 20 minutes so that the juices of the tomato and lettuce pool in the bottom of the bowl. Stir gently and eat with only the tangy juices for dressing.

However, in the middle of winter when all those expensive salad makings have a tired taste and cold weather is beginning to get irksome, a salad needs a tonic. This is my mid-winter formula. (I can never understand why I abhor in March the snow I so ecstatically welcome in November.)

In a small bowl combine honey with oil and vinegar. Beat with an egg beater until the mixture is very well blended (that means *all* the honey is mixed in) and frothy. Pour over the salad and toss. Try your taster on this dressing as you beat it—some taste buds like more oil or vinegar and some like more honey.

HELP YOURSELF SALAD PLATE
(SERVES FOUR TO SIX)

Dinner once on a meadow before a cabin on the beautiful Oregon coast blended elements of the West into a memorable evening. There were big prawns from the sea that we peeled and dipped with dripping fingers into melted garlic butter; an enormous do-it-yourself salad platter; homemade bread and hot coffee and even a California wine made of grapes and sunlight to sip; and an overall attitude of Western easy generosity and hospitality as big as the land.

SALAD: On a large platter arrange piles of torn lettuce, cucumber spears, sliced tomatoes, green pepper rings, sliced celery, raw cauliflower, avocado wedges, whole green onions, and whatever else you think might be good. Serve with a pitcher or bowl of the dressing, and let guests serve themselves according to whim.

DRESSING:

1	10 ¾-oz. can tomato soup, undiluted
¾	cup sugar
⅔	cup vinegar
2	tablespoons Worcestershire sauce
1	teaspoon salt
1½	cups salad oil
½	teaspoon dry mustard
1	clove garlic

Combine ingredients in a quart jar with a tightly fitting lid. Shake well. Store in refrigerator until needed. The dressing keeps well under refrigeration. Be careful not to accidentally pour the garlic clove onto someone's portion—as I once did to my husband, Tom—and be sure to remove the dressing from the refrigerator about ½ hour before serving. The flavors are improved when the dressing is close to room temperature. Shake or stir well before using.

CROW'S NEST SALAD
(SERVES SIX)

This salad, with toasted, homemade whole wheat bread, is a delicious summer luncheon or, with the addition of a soup, is an easy, relaxed dinner . . . and a favorite at the house called The Crow's Nest.

1	*small head very crisp lettuce, torn into bite-sized pieces*
1	*cup washed spinach leaves, torn into pieces*
1	*cucumber, pared and thinly sliced*
½	*cup thinly sliced unpeeled zucchini*
1	*cup ripe pitted olives*
½	*cup diced cheddar cheese*
½	*cup ham, salami, or leftover chicken, cut in thin strips*
4	*to 6 fresh mushrooms, thickly sliced*
1	*slice whole wheat bread, toasted and cubed*
1	*ripe tomato, diced*
1	*green pepper, sliced*
½	*cup coarsely chopped raw cauliflower*
¼	*cup hulled sunflower seeds*
1	*avocado, chopped*

Combine ingredients in a very large bowl. Sprinkle lightly with salt. Pour over ingredients ¾ to 1 cup dressing listed under GREEN SALAD earlier in this chapter. Toss to coat all ingredients. Also nice in this salad are chilled, cooked asparagus spears and quartered hard-cooked eggs.

DON'T FORGET THE VEGETABLES

To be truthful, old-time Westerners were not overly fond of vegetables. A meal wasn't a meal without meat, and meat usually meant only one thing—beef. I don't want to start the old cow versus sheep war all over again, but I must admit that my grandfather wouldn't allow lamb in the house and thought pork meant breakfast food.

The old cowboys loved fruit and enjoyed salads, and often carried canned tomatoes even when riding the range. They drank the juice for a thirst quencher, then ate the tomatoes to satisfy a vitamin craving. Every meal included meat and potatoes, and beans were an everyday staple. Vegetables were just not with it, and frontier cooks had to touch vegetables with a little imagination. The exception was corn on the cob.

The vegetable ideas and recipes that follow are either adaptations of old originals or come unchanged from family cooks on the Idaho frontier. (You can find ordinary directions and recipes for vegetables in other cookbooks.)

STRING BEANS

I don't think I have ever understood the difference between "green beans" and "string beans." "String beans" sounds a lot more interesting. Drain a #303 can of them and reserve the liquid for soups. Put beans in a saucepan and add ½ cup of either the GREEN SALAD dressing or WINTER DOLDRUMS SALAD dressing previously listed in this chapter. Heat through. Try this with canned peas and they will be substantially improved.

STRING BEANS IN SAUCE

When you have 1 lonely leftover frankfurter or link sausage, drain the liquid off a #303 can of string beans. With the liquid make a thin white sauce, or open a can of cream of mushroom soup to use as a sauce. Slice the frankfurter thinly, add it to the sauce, and stir mixture into the drained beans. Add salt and pepper to taste and heat through.

BEETS HARVARD

Mix ½ cup sugar with 1 tablespoon cornstarch in a small saucepan. Add ¼ cup water and ⅓ cup vinegar, and bring to a boil. Reduce heat immediately and simmer, stirring, until sauce has thickened. Add 5 whole cloves. Add 1 #303 can of drained sliced beets. Let stand 10 minutes, reheat, and serve.

BEETS YALE

Heat contents of 1 #303 can of sliced beets. Add 3 tablespoons butter or margarine, 3 tablespoons sugar, ½ teaspoon salt, and ¼ teaspoon prepared mustard. Stir well and heat until bubbly.

BEETS UNIVERSITY OF MONTANA!

Drain 1 #303 can sliced beets. Place beets in a shallow bowl. Slice a peeled onion thinly and add to beets. Repeat with a peeled cucumber. Pour over them just enough vinegar, or oil and vinegar dressing, to cover their tops. Season with salt and pepper. Chill 1 hour.

CRUMBY CABBAGE
(SERVES FOUR)

Coarsely shred 1 small cabbage and soak in cold salted water for 10 minutes. Bring to a boil, cover, reduce heat, and simmer 10 minutes. Drain well. Make 1 cup medium white sauce and blend into cabbage. Pour into buttered casserole dish, and add salt and pepper to taste. Sprinkle with paprika and top with ⅓ cup saltine cracker crumbs blended with 2 tablespoons melted butter or margarine. Bake at 350° F. for 10 minutes or until lightly browned.

CABBAGE CASSEROLE
(SERVES FOUR)

¼   *cup butter or margarine*
2   *tablespoons flour*
1   *#303 can tomatoes, mashed*
1   *small head cabbage, coarsely shredded*
1   *small onion, peeled and chopped*
2   *teaspoons salt*
¼   *teaspoon pepper*
¼   *cup white wine (optional)*

Melt butter in a heavy skillet. Add flour and stir until well mixed. Add tomatoes gradually, stirring constantly. Bring to a boil, add remaining ingredients, and stir to blend. Cover, reduce heat, and simmer slowly 45 minutes.

CANDY CARROTS
(SERVES FOUR TO SIX)

1   *pound carrots, scraped and thickly sliced*
½   *cup butter or margarine*
½   *cup brown sugar*
    shake cinnamon

Cook carrots in boiling water until tender—about 25 minutes. Drain. Melt butter in a heavy skillet and add brown sugar. Sprinkle with cinnamon and stir until smooth. Add carrots and cook over low heat, stirring constantly, until carrots are covered with glaze.

SILLY CELERY
(SERVES FOUR)

1   *medium bunch celery, cut into 2-inch lengths*
1½ *cups medium white sauce or 1 10 ¾-oz. can cream of celery soup*
    plus ½ can milk
1   *teaspoon salt*
¼   *teaspoon paprika*
    generous dash pepper

Cook celery in small amount of water until tender—10 to 15 minutes. Drain. Reheat in seasoned sauce or soup.

CORN OYSTERS
(SERVES FOUR)

1   *#303 can whole kernel corn, drained*
½   *cup soft bread crumbs*
1   *teaspoon salt*
¼   *teaspoon chili powder*
    dash pepper
1   *egg, beaten until frothy*

Combine corn with bread crumbs, add seasonings, and mix well. Beat egg and blend into corn mixture. Carefully drop by spoonsful onto a hot, greased griddle. Turn when golden and fry other side to match.

CORN PIE

(SERVES FOUR)

1¼   cups fine saltine cracker crumbs
½   cup melted butter or margarine
1¼   cups milk
1   #303 can whole kernel corn, drained
½   teaspoon salt
¼   teaspoon pepper
1   tablespoon minced green onion
2   tablespoons flour
2   eggs, beaten
     paprika

Mix crumbs with melted butter. Reserve ½ cup crumb mixture and press remainder into a 9-inch pie pan to form a shell. In a saucepan mix 1 cup milk, corn, salt, pepper, and onion. Simmer 3 minutes. Blend flour with ¼ cup milk and stir into hot mixture. Cook, stirring, until thickened. Cool slightly. Add beaten eggs slowly, beating with enthusiasm all the while. Pour into crumb-lined pan and sprinkle with reserved crumbs. Dash over the top with a shake of paprika. Bake in a hot (450° F.) oven for 15 minutes. Cut into wedges to serve.

COOKED LETTUCE

(SERVES FOUR)

1   large head lettuce, cut into eighths
⅓   cup butter or margarine
1   teaspoon salt
     dash pepper
     dash garlic powder

Cook lettuce in 1 cup salted water, covered, at a fast simmer for 5 minutes. Drain. Mix butter and seasonings in a heavy skillet. Melt butter over low heat. Add drained lettuce and simmer 15 minutes.

CREAMED ONIONS
(SERVES SIX)

4   *or 5 medium onions, peeled and halved*
1   *cup thin white sauce*
1   *teaspoon salt*
    dash pepper
½   *cup cracker crumbs mixed with 2 tablespoons melted butter*

Simmer halved onions in small amount of salted water until just tender. Drain, handling gently, and place in a buttered casserole dish, cut sides up. Cover with white sauce and season. Sprinkle with crumbs and bake at 350° F. for 15 minutes.

STUFFED ONIONS

Peel 1 large flattish onion for each serving. Steam for 30 minutes, or until just tender. Turn upside down and drain well 5 minutes, handling gently. When cool enough to handle, remove centers, saving to use in other recipes, and fill cavities with bread dressing, sautéed sausage, or leftover diced ham mixed with chopped tomato. Place stuffed onions closely together in a casserole dish and pour a cup of water around the onions. Sprinkle with salt, pepper, and ½ cup cracker crumbs mixed with 2 tablespoons melted butter. Cover and bake in a 350° F. oven until done—about 25 minutes. Uncover during last 10 minutes of baking so tops will brown.

SPINACH EVEN KIDS (AND I) WILL TRY
(SERVES FOUR)

2   *cups cooked spinach, drained and chopped*
2   *eggs, well beaten*
½   *cup cracker crumbs*
1   *teaspoon salt*
2   *teaspoons lemon juice*
3   *tablespoons finely minced onion*

Combine ingredients and mix together. Drop gently by rounded table-spoonsful onto hot, well-greased griddle and fry gently. Turn and fry other side. Drain on paper toweling and serve hot. If you are hurried, combine ingredients, stir well, pour into a well-greased casserole dish, and bake at 350° F. for 25 minutes.

TOMATO CASSEROLE
(SERVES FOUR TO SIX)

My mother's volatile sister, Betty, is a fine cook in the lavish, hospitable tradition of the West. The celebration of life with food and laughter came down undiminished through the generations of my family to her. Marvelous things roll out of her kitchen—lasagne; cabbage salad with shrimp and bits of purple onion in it; veal scallopini; five-layer cakes with frosting on top, sides, between layers, *and on the bottom*; and a splendid stew fondly named Son-of-a-Bitch. One of my favorites of all her recipes is TOMATO CASSEROLE.

1	*#2½ can tomatoes*
1½	*teaspoons salt*
¼	*teaspoon pepper*
1	*small onion, peeled and chopped finely*
½	*cup cracker crumbs mixed with 2 tablespoons melted butter or margarine*
½	*cup shredded cheddar cheese*

Mix tomatoes, seasonings, and onion, and set aside. Mix buttered cracker crumbs with cheese. Put half of the tomato mixture in a buttered casserole and top with half of the crumb mixture. Repeat. Bake at 350° F. for 30 minutes.

VEGETABLE FRITTERS

You can make fritters out of almost any vegetable. Sliced tomatoes are marvelous—especially green tomatoes. (The first time I served fried green tomatoes I made the mistake of frying only 4 tomatoes—and the platter was empty by the time it got to me.) Sliced zucchini and eggplant are great as fritters; fried asparagus is exceptional; even turnips and carrots are delicious.

To fritter tomatoes, zucchini, and eggplant, slice in ⅛- to ¼-inch slices. To prepare for 4 people, beat 2 eggs slightly with 1 teaspoon water. Roll saltine crackers with your rolling pin to make 2 cups crumbs. Dip vegetable slices in crumbs, then in egg, and a second time in crumbs. Fry until browned in ¼-inch hot fat in a heavy skillet. Season lightly with salt, turn, and fry other side. Drain on paper toweling and serve hot.

For cauliflower, soak head of cauliflower for 30 minutes in cold, salted water. Drain, and cook in fresh water 15 minutes. Drain again, and separate into flowers. Dip flowers in egg and then in cracker crumbs, and fry in hot fat until golden.

Asparagus must be simmered 15 minutes, drained gently, then dipped first in egg, then in crumbs, and again in egg. Fry in hot fat until golden.

String beans, wax beans, carrots, turnips, and parsnips should be pre-cooked until tender before frying. For 2 cups of these vegetables make a batter of 1 slightly beaten egg, ⅔ cup milk, 1 tablespoon oil, 1 cup flour, and 1 teaspoon salt. (Adjust the thickness of batter by increasing or decreasing the amount of flour.) Stir until smooth. Dip the vegetable by slotted spoonsful into the batter, then slip into ¼-inch hot fat in a heavy skillet or fry on a hot, well-greased griddle. Fry until lightly browned, turn carefully, and fry on other side. Drain on paper toweling and serve hot.

CHILLED VEGETABLE PLATE

The country around Big Creek, deep in the rugged fastness of the Idaho Primitive Area where wildness is satisfyingly vast, is a homeland for wild animals now seen only in the West. We've watched mountain lions there—the big, incredibly graceful cats variously called puma, painter, panther, and cougar, with their serene, Oriental faces. On trails there we've heard the lovely little questioning sound they make, similar to a tiny bell. On Big Creek we've seen Rocky Mountain bighorn sheep—rams with massive, curved horns, and tidy-bodied ewes—and have succumbed to their captivating, quixotic personalities. There are coyotes, weasel, deer, elk, and shiny-coated bear. We spent one delightful afternoon laughing over the antics of a pair of otter—pert and gay and bright.

No roads penetrate the primitive country from the outside. Trails are long and arduous, and during our weeks there on a wildlife photo expedition our supplies were delivered by bush plane to a landing strip a mile from our camp. Our life-style and attitudes were uncluttered and uncomplicated, and we learned to savor simple things. One of our favorite dinners consisted of trout caught in the Middle Fork of the Salmon River, served with toasted, homemade bread and this lavish assortment of vegetables.

In individual bowls marinate well-drained, cooked vegetables—string beans, asparagus, sliced broccoli stems, thin strips of carrots, sliced or small whole beets, and peas—in any of the 3 dressings in the salad section (listed under GREEN SALAD, WINTER DOLDRUMS SALAD, or HELP YOURSELF SALAD PLATE). In other bowls marinate raw onion rings and cauliflower flowers. Chill for at least 1 hour and then drain, accumulating dressings in a jar to use on another mixed-greens salad on another day. Serve chilled, marinated vegetables arranged in separate heaps on a platter. Garnish with quartered tomatoes and halved hard-cooked eggs.

If a dressing is desired, serve a bowl of roquefort dressing or 1 cup of mayonnaise thinned with ¼ cup salad oil and 1 tablespoon vinegar, stirred until blended, with a dash of pepper and a pinch of dry mustard, or with a cruet of the same dressing you used as a marinade.

AUTUMN ZUCCHINI
(SERVES FOUR TO SIX)

In the fall the skies of the West echo with the heart-gripping call of wild Canada geese—honkers, heading south. They trace long, undulating lines and wavering V's, high and free. Their faint, triumphant clamor drifts earthward, and something dormant in the tamed spirit of man recognizes it and responds.

One autumn evening I was pulling zucchini in the garden for this recipe when I heard geese far overhead. I stood, grubby and rooted, listening to the wild exultance in the sky, and felt a nameless yearning. Perhaps I like zucchini so much because I remember wild geese calling.

6   *cups peeled and finely chopped zucchini*
1   *onion, peeled and shredded*
1   *stalk celery, minced*
1   *clove garlic, mashed*
3   *cups soft bread crumbs*
½   *cup shredded Monterey Jack or mild cheddar cheese*
     salt and pepper

Cook zucchini in small amount of salted water 7 minutes. Drain well. Combine with remaining ingredients, season to taste, and stir until well blended. Gently drop by large spoonsful into about ¼ inch of hot fat in a heavy skillet. Fry until golden, turn, and fry other side. Serve with a teaspoon of sauce on each of the patties.

SAUCE:
2   *tablespoons butter or margarine*
2   *tablespoons flour*
2   *cups tomato juice or 1 16-oz. can tomato sauce*
3   *tablespoons minced, peeled onion*
     salt and pepper
     pinch cinnamon

Melt butter and blend in flour in a small saucepan. Add tomato juice, stirring constantly, and cook over a low heat until thickened. Add remaining ingredients and simmer gently, stirring frequently, 15 minutes.

Chapter 9

THE SWEET TOOTH WAY TO LEAVE THE TABLE FEELING FULL

The West always did have a sweet tooth. In the early days, chuck wagon cooks and homestead women made jams and jellies out of wild fruits, and candies and cookies for treats. My grandfather carried thick, white peppermints in his pocket, and the penny-candy display cases in small-town stores were feature attractions for children.

Pioneers trudging west carefully carried the tender shoots of familiar fruit trees with them. As soon as they had built shelter for themselves and their animals, they planted gardens and cleared land for their small family orchards, and waited for the brave little twigs to bear fruit.

Today, crabbed old orchards long past their fruitful days linger in neat patches, outliving log cabins and barns, and often miles from any indication that men had ever passed that way. A few trees in once-tidy rows, a fragment of fence, and a shred of foundation stone are often all that is left to mark where a nameless pioneer won or lost—and yet I think those stalwart pioneers have left honorable signatures upon the land.

The trees were usually apple, as hardy and stubborn as the people themselves. The women used the fruit in ways that are delicious to families today.

FRONTIER FRUIT DESSERTS

APPLE CRISP
(SERVES FOUR)

1   cup all-purpose flour
1   cup sugar
1   teaspoon baking powder
1   tablespoon cinnamon
1   egg, slightly beaten
6   large apples, peeled and thinly sliced
4   tablespoons butter or margarine

Mix flour with sugar, baking powder, and cinnamon. Add egg and stir until mixture is crumbly. Cover bottom of a greased 2 quart casserole with apple slices and spread the crumb mixture over the top. Melt butter and drizzle over the crumbs. Bake at 350° F. until done—about 40 minutes.

APPLE CRUMBLE
(SERVES FOUR)

4   cups peeled and sliced tart apples
½   cup water
¾   cup all-purpose flour, unsifted
1   cup white sugar or ½ cup white sugar and ½ cup brown sugar, packed
1   teaspoon cinnamon
½   cup butter or margarine

Arrange apple slices in a buttered 2-quart baking dish. Pour water over. With a fork, blend flour with sugar, cinnamon, and butter. Stir into apples. Bake at 350° F. for 30 minutes.

APPLE CRUNCH
(SERVES FOUR)

2   *eggs*
1   *cup sugar*
⅔   *cup sifted all-purpose flour*
¼   *teaspoon salt*
2½   *teaspoons baking powder*
1   *cup chopped unpeeled tart apples*
2   *teaspoons vanilla*

Beat eggs with sugar. Add flour, salt, and baking powder. Stir in apples and vanilla. Pour into a greased 7½″ × 9″ baking dish and bake at 350° F. for 30 minutes.

APPLE DANDY
(SERVES FOUR)

4   *tart apples, peeled and sliced thinly*
½   *cup sugar*
½   *teaspoon cinnamon*
¾   *teaspoon salt*
¼   *cup molasses*
½   *cup hot water*
1   *cup sifted all-purpose flour*
1½   *teaspoons baking powder*
⅓   *cup lard or shortening*
⅓   *cup milk*

Put apple slices in a 7½″ × 9″ oblong baking dish. Mix sugar with cinnamon and ¼ teaspoon salt, and sprinkle over apples. Combine molasses and hot water, and pour over apples. Bake in a hot (400° F.) oven for 25 minutes. Mix flour with baking powder and ½ teaspoon salt, and cut in lard with a pastry cutter. Stir in milk. Knead lightly, roll into rectangle ⅓-inch thick and fit over apples. Prick top with a fork and bake at 400° F. for 20 to 25 minutes.

JOAN LE FEVRE'S APPLE ROLL
(SERVES FOUR TO SIX)

My grandmother was a pretty, blue-eyed Idaho girl of gentleness and humor when my grandfather met her. He was a carefree bachelor cowboy, not quite sure he was through sowing his wild oats; and although he was deeply in love with her, he ran out on their engagement and went clear to Texas to "forget" her. She "forgot" him by promptly getting herself engaged to a promising young man-about-town, and was strolling down Main Street with her fiancé when my grandfather rode back into town to find the woman he couldn't forget. He rode his horse up beside her and said simply, "Joan, I'm back." She never bothered to say good-bye to her gentlemanly fiancé, but went to my grandfather without a backward glance.

She wrote her recipe for apple roll on the back of the envelope that held their wedding certificate.

2	cups biscuit dough, from any standard recipe or biscuit mix, with 1 tablespoon white sugar added
2	cups grated pared apples
1	cup white sugar
1	tablespoon butter or margarine
½	cup brown sugar
⅛	teaspoon cinnamon
½	teaspoon nutmeg
2	cups boiling water

Roll biscuit dough out as for pie crust, into an oblong shape. Make a filling of the apples, ¼ cup white sugar, and butter, and spread evenly over dough. Roll up as for jelly roll and slice into 1½-inch slices. In an ovenproof baking dish combine ¾ cup white sugar, ½ cup brown sugar, cinnamon, nutmeg, and hot water. Bring to a boil on top burner. Gently add apple roll slices and put dish in a preheated 350° F. oven 30 minutes or until brown.

Serve warm, plain or with cream.

nutmeg

BAKED APPLES

Core firm, tart apples and put bottom down in a baking dish. Fill cavities with a sugar-spice mixture, allowing ¼ cup sugar and a pinch cinnamon for each apple. Add 1 teaspoon butter or margarine to each cavity. Cover bottom of baking pan with boiling water and bake at 400° F. 30 to 45 minutes or until apples are soft. Baste often with syrup in the pan.

Serve warm, alone or with milk.

BAKED PEACHES

Where the climate permitted, homesteaders in the West planted peach trees beside their apples. Frontier women canned the golden fruit in quart jars to open during bitter winter days.

Arrange canned peach halves, hollow up, in a shallow baking dish allowing 2 halves per person. Pour a little of the peach syrup over each peach half, and sprinkle with brown sugar and a dash of cinnamon. Bake about 20 minutes in a 350° oven, or broil 4 inches from heat for 5 minutes. Serve hot.

BAKED ORANGES
(SERVES EIGHT)

Today's people take oranges for granted, and they are available year-round in all parts of the country. For frontier families it was a different story. Oranges were treasures, bought when there was a little extra cash on hand, considered rare and exotic. One of the golden treats went into each child's Christmas stocking; and if enough oranges were left over, the mammas baked an elegant Christmas dessert like this:

4   *large oranges*
     sugar
     butter or margarine
2   *teaspoons cornstarch*
½   *cup water (from water oranges cooked in)*
½   *cup orange juice*

Cover oranges with boiling water and cook until skins are tender when pricked with a fork. Drain, reserving water, cut in halves, and core. Put in a baking dish and fill centers with sugar. Sprinkle sugar over tops. Dot with margarine. Heat under broiler until sugar melts and turns golden. Make a sauce by stirring cornstarch into a mixture of the water and orange juice. Cook and stir 3 minutes, or until sauce is thickened. Pour over oranges. Serve warm.

FRUIT FRITTERS

My Scotch great-grandmother made fritters out of anything—and her fritters were unlike any others I have ever tasted. Instead of including fruit in a batter and making little fried cakes, she dipped fruit in a batter and fried the coated fruit in hot fat.

I have tried her method on peeled, cored apples cut in ½-inch rings; bananas cut into halves lengthwise; drained, canned peach halves and peeled, halved fresh peaches dredged lightly in flour first; and orange sections.

For 3 cups fruit, make a batter by mixing: 2 slightly beaten eggs with ⅔ cup milk, 1 tablespoon oil or melted butter, 1½ cups flour, ¼ teaspoon salt, and 2 tablespoons sugar.

Heat 1 inch of fat or cooking oil in a heavy skillet until hot enough to brown a cube of bread in 1 minute. Put fruit in batter, remove with a long-handled fork and carefully lower into fat. Fry until golden—about 3 minutes—remove, and drain. Sprinkle with powdered sugar while hot.

BAKED FRUIT COCKTAIL
(SERVES FOUR)

Drain a large can of fruit cocktail. Put in a baking dish and sprinkle generously with brown sugar. Bake at 350° F. for 20 minutes.

COOKIES

I don't remember many cookies from my childhood. My grandmother and my mother after her were not much for making cookies—they turned out pies and cakes with deft hands, but cookies were not in the forefront of their cookery imaginations.

I do remember BOILED COOKIES, rich and chewy and as good as little pieces of cake. There were SUGAR COOKIES for dunking in cold milk or hot tea, and a Western adaptation of macaroons that was my favorite.

BOILED COOKIES
(MAKES 4 DOZEN)

2	cups sugar
3	tablespoons cocoa
½	cup butter or margarine
½	cup milk
½	cup peanut butter
3	cups uncooked rolled oats

Combine in saucepan sugar, cocoa, butter, and milk. Bring to a boil and cook 2 minutes. Add remaining ingredients and stir well. Drop by teaspoonful onto waxed paper. Cool.

WESTERN MACAROONS
(MAKES 2 DOZEN)

1	egg white, beaten stiff
½	cup sugar
½	cup shredded coconut
1	cup cornflakes
½	teaspoon almond flavoring
½	teaspoon vanilla
	dash salt

Combine ingredients in order given and mix together well. Drop from the tip of a spoon onto a buttered cookie sheet and bake at 350° F. about 20 minutes.

SUGAR COOKIES
(MAKES NEARLY 100)

I remember these cookies best from Christmases when some loving and loved family cook sprinkled them with red sugar before baking to lift them into the holiday mood.

1 *cup butter or margarine*
1 *cup cooking oil*
2 *eggs*
1 *cup confectioners' sugar*
1 *cup granulated sugar*
4 *cups all-purpose flour*
1 *teaspoon salt*
1 *teaspoon baking soda*
1 *teaspoon cream of tartar*
1 *teaspoon vanilla*
¼ *cup very finely chopped walnut meats*

Cream together butter, oil, and eggs, then add sugars and blend well together. Sift together flour, salt, baking soda, and cream of tartar and add to cookie mixture. Beat well and add vanilla and nuts. Drop by teaspoonsful onto a greased cookie sheet. Bake at 375° F. for 8 minutes.

CAKES

Cakes were appreciated for the special productions they really were in the days before they became premixed, instant, and packaged. Most of these cake recipes are old hand-me-downs, adapted to present ingredients and methods, and a few are from the turn of the century or before—even the adaptations are in some cases at least thirty years old.

EVERYDAY CAKE

A birthday or "company" cake was put on a pretty plate and frosted all the way around. An "everyday" cake was usually a sheet cake, frosted in the pan and therefore frosted only on top.

⅓	cup cocoa
1	cup water
⅔	cup shortening
2½	cups sifted all-purpose flour
1	teaspoon baking soda
1	teaspoon salt
1½	teaspoons cinnamon
2	cups sugar
2	eggs
½	cup buttermilk
1	teaspoon vanilla

Mix cocoa and water in a saucepan, and add shortening. Bring mixture to a boil, turn off heat, and cool slightly. Sift together flour, baking soda, salt, and cinnamon. Blend together sugar and eggs in a large mixing bowl and blend in cocoa mixture. (Do not beat.) Add sifted dry ingredients alternately with buttermilk, stirring after each addition until well blended. Stir in vanilla. Pour into greased, flat cake pan (15" ×10" × 1") or jelly roll pan. Bake in a 400° F. oven for 20 minutes. Cool.

FROSTING:

½	cup butter or margarine
¼	cup milk
¼	cup cocoa
3	cups sifted confectioners' sugar
1	teaspoon vanilla
½	cup chopped nuts

Melt butter in small saucepan and add milk. Mix cocoa with sugar and stir into milk. Add vanilla and nuts. Blend together. Spread on cake.

HAY DAY CAKE

On the ranch in Idaho called The Hat, wild hay grew all by itself, seeding itself from itself in the wind, watered by a miraculous water table that percolated through the soil and subirrigated the land. The hay had only to be cut and piled into high haystacks to feed the livestock through the winter. On hay day, when the hands came and everybody pitched in to get the haying done, my grandmother and her sisters and neighbors gathered in the kitchen before daybreak and cooked all day long. My grandmother often served this cake, so similar to German Chocolate that I wonder where she got the recipe.

1	*cup oats, the quick-cook variety*
1	*stick butter or margarine*
1	*cup brown sugar*
1½	*cups boiling water*
1	*cup white sugar*
1½	*cups all-purpose flour*
3	*tablespoons cocoa*
½	*teaspoon salt*
1	*teaspoon baking soda*
3	*eggs*

Combine first 4 ingredients in mixing bowl. Cover and let sit 30 minutes. Then sift together dry ingredients and add to mixture in bowl. Beat eggs slightly and add. Stir well together. Pour into a greased 9″ × 12″ baking pan and bake 35 minutes at 350° F. Cool slightly before adding topping.

TOPPING:

1	*cup brown sugar*
1	*teaspoon vanilla*
½	*cup shredded cocoanut*
½	*cup butter or margarine*
1	*cup chopped nuts*
3	*tablespoons evaporated milk*

Combine ingredients in a saucepan and heat over low setting until mixture melts together. Spread topping over still-warm cake and pop into oven or under broiler until the top bubbles.

SILLY CAKE

I knew this cake always as SILLY CAKE, but I have been told that it is also known as Crazy Cake and is not native to the West. All recipes that were not invented in the West came from someplace else first—but the pioneers lived someplace else first, too, and they probably brought this recipe with them.

3	cups all-purpose flour
2	cups sugar
1	teaspoon salt
2	teaspoons baking soda
6	tablespoons cocoa
2	cups water
½	cup cooking oil
2	tablespoons vinegar
1½	teaspoons vanilla

Sift together dry ingredients. Add remaining ingredients and beat well. Pour into a greased 9″ × 12″ baking pan and bake at 350° F. for 40 minutes. Frost with a butter frosting while cake is still in the pan.

EASY CAKE

1	egg, beaten
½	cup sugar
1	cup all-purpose flour
1	teaspoon baking powder
¼	teaspoon salt
¼	cup milk
3	tablespoons melted butter
1	teaspoon vanilla

Beat egg and add sugar while beating. Add flour that has been sifted with baking powder and salt. Add milk, melted butter, and vanilla, and stir well. Bake 25 minutes in a 350° F. oven in a greased and floured 7″ × 10″ pan. Serve with Vanilla Sauce poured over individual servings.

VANILLA SAUCE:

½   *cup sugar*
1   *tablespoon cornstarch*
1   *cup boiling water*
2   *teaspoons vanilla*
    pinch of salt

Mix sugar and cornstarch together and add boiling water gradually, stirring constantly. Boil 15 minutes. Remove from heat, add vanilla and salt, and stir well.

JAM-DANDY CAKE

This very old cake recipe must have satisfied all the needs of pioneer cooking. The ingredients are simple and inexpensive, the procedure is short and easy, and it is a very good cake. Use any kind of jam.

¾   *cup shortening*
1   *cup jam*
½   *cup buttermilk*
3   *eggs*
1   *cup sugar*
1½ *cups all-purpose flour*
1   *teaspoon baking soda*
1   *teaspoon ground cloves*
½   *teaspoon cinnamon*
½   *teaspoon nutmeg*

Cream well together shortening, jam, buttermilk, and eggs. Sift in sugar, flour, baking soda, and spices. Mix well until thick and light. Pour into greased and floured 9″ × 12″ pan. Bake at 350° F. for 45 minutes. Glaze while still hot.

GLAZE:

Boil until clear ¾ cup sugar and 3 tablespoons lemon juice. Pour over hot cake. Allow to cool completely before cutting cake.

CARROT CAKE

If this is not the very best carrot cake recipe in the West, I'd like to taste the one that is. It is very rich, and you will want to serve smaller cake portions than usual.

I found this cake in a little hamlet named Gibbonsville, in Idaho. Gibbonsville must be one of the loveliest historic towns of the West, settled in a narrow, winding, wooded valley between two high mountain ridges that encircle it like arms. Placer miners established a camp at Gibbonsville in 1872; and by 1879, the first stamp mill was built there. By 1896, it was the largest settlement in Lemhi County, quite an accomplishment considering that Salmon City, thirty-three miles south, was getting a lot of attention as a frontier town. In keeping with the often one-sided value standards of the old West, the town was named after Colonel John Gibbon, who massacred Nez Perce women and children just over the mountain from Gibbonsville in 1877.

Gibbonsville is still there, lovely and nearly a ghost town with its twelve families. They are clannish people to whom a newcomer is still a newcomer after twenty years and who view change with suspicion. There are old log buildings and trees and fences and meadows, and Dahlonega Creek murmurs through the valley. Coyotes sing across the big meadow at the mouth of the valley, and there is a great horned owl living behind the old schoolhouse who will answer you if you answer him. On summer evenings peace floods the valley like moonlight.

1½	cups cooking oil
2	cups sugar
4	eggs
2	teaspoons baking soda
1	teaspoon salt
2	teaspoons baking powder
2	teaspoons cinnamon
2	cups sifted all-purpose flour
2	teaspoons vanilla
3	cups grated scraped carrots
1	cup chopped walnut meats

Mix oil and sugar together until blended. Add eggs one at a time, mixing each egg in before adding the next. Sift dry ingredients together and add to sugar and oil mixture. Stir in grated carrots and nuts. Mix well. Batter will be very thick. Bake in a 10″ × 14″ oblong cake pan in a 375° F. oven for about 40 minutes, or until a toothpick inserted in the center comes out clean.

ICING:

1   *8-oz. package softened cream cheese*
1   *1-pound package powdered sugar*
½   *cup melted butter or margarine*
2   *teaspoons vanilla*

Mix ingredients together and whip like whipped cream. If too stiff to whip after a few moments, add a bit more melted butter. Frost cake when cooled, and cut into smallish squares to serve.

VICTORY CAKE

This cake came out of the tense years of World War II. It isn't essentially western and it is only as old as that war, but it was baked in the West and still is.

1   *cup mayonnaise or salad dressing*
1   *cup sugar*
1   *teaspoon vanilla*
2   *cups all-purpose flour*
4   *tablespoons cocoa*
2   *teaspoons baking soda*
     pinch salt
1   *cup strong coffee*

Mix together first 3 ingredients. Sift together next 4 ingredients. Combine the 2 groups alternately with coffee. Bake in a 9″ × 9″ cake pan about 40 minutes in a 350° F. oven.

TOM'S CAKE

This was the first birthday cake I ever baked for my husband. It's a good bride's cake—easy to make and impressively good.

I don't know that it was a bride's cake in the old West, but it was baked there long ago. It is similar to HAY DAY CAKE, and may have been a variation invented when the pantry was out of cocoa.

1¼	cups boiling water
1	cup oatmeal
½	cup soft butter or margarine
1	cup granulated sugar
1	cup brown sugar
1	teaspoon vanilla
2	eggs
1½	cups all-purpose flour
1	teaspoon baking soda
½	teaspoon salt
¾	teaspoon cinnamon
¼	teaspoon nutmeg

Pour boiling water over oatmeal and let stand 20 minutes. Mix remaining ingredients into oatmeal and stir well. Pour into a 9-inch square pan and bake at 325° F. for 50 minutes.

FROSTING:

¼	cup butter, melted
½	cup brown sugar
3	tablespoons cream
½	cup chopped nuts
¾	cup coconut

Combine all ingredients and stir well together. Spread over cake. Broil 5 inches from heat until top is bubbly. The cake is supposed to cool before serving, but my family rarely wants to wait that long.

WYOMING NUTBREAD

The Jackson Hole country of Wyoming is one of those favored places on the face of the earth that is so lovely that people like me can gawk and look and trip over their feet without apology. The Teton Range rises in majesty to the west of the valley, so high and jagged that it isn't quite believable. The Snake River winds from lake to lake and is joined by the Gros Ventre just above the little town of Wilson.

I found this old-fashioned nut bread in Jackson Hole, accompanied by tea stirred with a peppermint stick.

3	*cups sifted all-purpose flour*
1	*cup granulated sugar*
4	*teaspoons baking powder*
½	*teaspoon cinnamon*
2	*teaspoons salt*
1	*egg, slightly beaten*
¼	*cup shortening, melted*
1½	*cups milk*
1	*teaspoon vanilla*
1½	*cups chopped walnuts*

Resift flour with sugar, baking powder, cinnamon, and salt. Add egg, shortening, milk, and vanilla. Stir until all of the dry ingredients are moistened. Stir in walnuts. Pour into a greased 9″ × 5″ × 3″ loaf pan, and bake at 350° F. for about 1 hour and 15 minutes, or until a toothpick inserted in the center comes out clean.

FROSTINGS

Any one of these old frosting recipes is superlative on just about any cake. Put FRENCH CREAM FROSTING on a vanilla or chocolate cake, spread ORANGE FROSTING on a vanilla or spice cake, top any cake with WALNUT GLAZE.

At county fairs throughout the West, all the good cooks around trek to the fairgrounds with their best cakes—vying for the blue ribbon and a two-dollar prize. One lady in a Montana farm town made all the other cooks nervous by baking the same prize-winning cake three years in a row and just changing the frosting each year. After three blue ribbons she moved away and everybody breathed a sign of relief.

These are her frostings:

FRENCH CREAM FROSTING

½   cup soft butter
2½   cups sifted powdered sugar
1   egg
2   squares unsweetened chocolate
1   teaspoon vanilla

Cream butter. Add sugar and egg and mix thoroughly. Blend in chocolate and vanilla. Beat until frosting is of spreading consistency.

ORANGE FROSTING

1   tablespoon strained orange juice
1   egg yolk, slightly beaten
1   cup powdered sugar
1   teaspoon salt

Combine juice slowly with egg yolk. Add powdered sugar and salt gradually, and beat constantly until mixture is of spreading consistency.

WALNUT GLAZE

1   *cup sifted powdered sugar*
2   *tablespoons butter or margarine*
6   *tablespoons cream*
½   *teaspoon vanilla*
½   *cup chopped walnuts*

Cream sugar with butter. Add remaining ingredients and mix well together. Pour over warm cake.

PIES

Settlers in the old West loved pies even more than they did cakes, and it was no wonder. When the women opened the oven doors of the big, wood-burning ranges, they lifted out pies done to a golden turn and made of the best their country and their skills had to offer.

All these pie recipes save one came from the kitchens of my people in Idaho—the one exception is RUSTIC RAISIN PIE, and that recipe is made by a friend who lives on the North Fork of Idaho's Salmon River.

RUSTIC RAISIN PIE

1   *cup orange juice*
3   *tablespoons lemon juice*
¾   *cup cold water*
½   *cup honey*
¼   *teaspoon salt*
3   *tablespoons cornstarch*
2   *cups seedless raisins*
1   *recipe pie pastry*
1   *tablespoon all-purpose flour*
1   *tablespoon butter or margarine*

Combine first 5 ingredients and heat to boiling. Mix cornstarch with a little cold water and blend into the hot mixture. Stir until thickened. Rinse raisins and stir into hot mixture. Remove from heat. Line pie pan with pastry and sprinkle with flour. Pour in filling, dot with butter, and cover with top crust. Cut 4 short slits in top crust. Bake in a 425° F. oven for 35 to 40 minutes.

CHESS PIE

One of my forebears was a cultured, wealthy gentleman from a Kentucky plantation. When he decided to go west, he did it in style.

He loaded all his possessions and his black slaves into big Conestoga wagons, but he and his wife rode in a fine buggy drawn by finely bred horses. He brought with him his stable of thoroughbred race horses, and probably a taste for good bourbon and mint juleps. When he reached the free states his slaves ran away—all but one who took care of his children and couldn't bring herself to leave them. In the middle of what is now Utah, an Indian raiding party ran off with all his prized horses. It was legend in the West for years that many a classy Indian pony could trace its lineage to those thoroughbreds from Kentucky.

Horses were not all they brought with them. There were lovely pieces of French cut glass, crystal goblets, a banquet-sized tablecloth edged with heavy satin-stitch, and a recipe for CHESS PIE.

2	cups sugar
1	tablespoon flour
½	pound butter or margarine
6	eggs
½	teaspoon vanilla
1	teaspoon grated lemon peel
1	unbaked pie shell
1	cup tart jelly, such as currant

Mix sugar and flour together and add butter. Blend and beat until light and fluffy. Add eggs one at a time, beating well after each addition. Add vanilla and lemon peel.

Spread jelly on the bottom of the pie crust. Top with pie filling. Bake at 300° F. for about an hour, or until a knife inserted in the center comes out clean. One of my neighbors says she makes CHESS PIE with the same ingredients and proportions, but her recipe differs in baking time—15 minutes at 500° F., then 15 additional minutes at 250° F.

NUT PIE

My grandfather was a cowboy. He drove a freight wagon into the old General Custer Mine near Challis, Idaho, when he was too little to handle the reins, and he rode roundup with men when he was so small that he needed a fence post or stump in order to climb into the saddle. His rough childhood matured him too soon, and he was a handful.

As a child he did dreadful, irreverent things like tieing his rope to outhouses and pulling them over with his horse, and riding a half-broken horse into a dance hall. He was sent to a boarding school and was promptly expelled for using the headmaster's hat for an indelicate purpose for which it had not been intended. His father was a proud old gentleman of fine family, and my grandfather must have been a headache for him. My great-grandfather was accustomed to the "finer things in life," and considered this pie one of them.

½   cup granulated sugar
1   cup dark corn syrup
3   eggs
4   tablespoons melted butter
1   teaspoon vanilla
1   cup chopped nuts—walnuts, pecans, almonds, or filberts
1   unbaked pie shell

Cook sugar with syrup until mixture thickens. Beat eggs well and slowly add hot syrup while beating steadily. Add melted butter, vanilla, and nuts. Pour into pie shell and bake at 450° F. for 10 minutes. Reduce heat to 300° F. and continue baking 35 minutes. Cool.

HAT RANCH PIE

My people no longer live on the Hat Ranch. It belongs to someone else now. Some other child calls the old, two-story log house "home," other feet wade in Antelope Creek and climb the huge rock that is shaped like a loaf of bread, and other ears listen to sage hen gadding about in the willows. I wonder if anyone there makes HAT RANCH PIE the way my grand-mother did. Her pastry is easy and foolproof, and a good one to know.

PIE PASTRY: (Divide recipe in half if you're making a single-crust pie.)

    2   cups sifted all-purpose flour
    1   teaspoon salt
    ⅔   cup shortening
    3   or 4 tablespoons cold water

Sift sifted flour and salt into a bowl; cut in shortening until mixture is crumbly. Sprinkle cold water over, a tablespoon at a time, and mix lightly with a fork just until the pastry holds together and leaves the side of the bowl clean. This makes enough for one 9-inch double-crust pie, or two 9-inch single-crust pies.

PIE FILLING:

    7   cups pared apples, cut into chunks
    ½   cup sugar
    2   tablespoons flour
    ½   teaspoon nutmeg
    ½   cup raisins
    ½   cup chopped walnuts
    2   tablespoons lemon juice

    ½   cup sugar
    ½   cup flour
    2   cups butter or margarine
    ½   cup chopped walnuts

Put apple chunks in a large bowl. Mix ½ cup sugar with 2 tablespoons flour, nutmeg, raisins, and ½ cup chopped walnuts. Sprinkle over apples and stir gently to coat, then spoon into an unbaked pie shell. Drizzle with lemon juice.

Mix ½ cup sugar and ½ cup flour in a small bowl. Cut in butter until mixture is crumbly. Stir in ½ cup walnuts and sprinkle mixture evenly over apples. Cover pie loosely with foil. Put on a large cookie sheet and bake in a hot (425° F.) oven for 1 hour. Remove from oven, lift off foil, and cool pie completely before cutting.

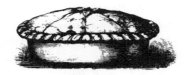

AUTUMN PIE

PASTRY:

1½	*cups sifted all-purpose flour*
½	*teaspoon salt*
⅓	*cup shortening*
½	*cup grated American cheese*
¼	*cup cold water*

Resift flour with salt into a large bowl. Cut in shortening until mixture is crumbly. Stir in cheese. Sprinkle cold water over, a tablespoon at a time, and mix lightly until pastry holds together. Roll out half of pastry on a floured board and fit into a 9-inch pie pan.

PIE FILLING:

1	*jar (1 lb., 12 oz.) prepared mincemeat*
2	*cups chopped apples*
1	*teaspoon brandy or apple cider*

Mix mincemeat with apples and brandy. Pour into unbaked pie shell. Roll out remaining pastry and fit over pie. Flute edges, trim off excess, and cut slits in top of pastry. Bake in a 425° F. oven for 45 minutes, or until pastry is golden. Cool completely before cutting.

CRUNCHY APPLE PIE

¼	teaspoon salt
¾	cup sugar
2	tablespoons flour
½	teaspoon cinnamon
¼	teaspoon ground cloves
½	teaspoon vanilla
2	teaspoons lemon juice
5½	cups thinly sliced tart apples
3	tablespoons melted butter or margarine
3	tablespoons chilled, chunk-style peanut butter
¼	cup sugar
½	cup coarsely crushed cornflakes
	pinch salt
1	unbaked pie shell

Combine first 8 ingredients and stir gently together until ingredients are well distributed. Spoon into pie shell and drizzle with melted butter.

Blend peanut butter with ¼ cup sugar, cornflakes, and salt with a pastry blender until crumbly. Sprinkle over apples. Bake in a 350° F. oven for 45 minutes to an hour.

ANGEL PIE

This pie and I don't get along together, and I don't know why. Everybody else in my family makes it frequently and never has a bit of trouble, but I do. The putting together of the ingredients isn't difficult, but sometimes it doesn't do what it is supposed to do in the oven. Still, the pie is so truly heavenly that it is well worth a serious try.

11	graham crackers
1	cup sugar
3	eggs, separated
1	teaspoon baking powder
¾	cup walnuts, chopped coarsely

Crush crackers and mix with sugar. Beat egg yolks and stir into cracker-sugar mixture. Stir in nuts and baking powder. Beat egg whites stiff and carefully fold into pie mixture. Spread in buttered pie pan. Bake 35 minutes in a slow (250° F.) oven. Open oven door and let pie cool in oven.

SOUR-CREAM PIE

One of my great-aunts was an auburn-haired belle of the ball every place she went, gay and gallant with a gift of laughter. She was the one who "wrote down" the old recipe for soured cream pie, and I love to read her beautiful handwriting flowing across the page.

This pie recipe is so old that its origins have been lost. It is at least sixty years old in the ranch country of Idaho, and how many years it has lived beyond that I do not know. It is rich and marvelous and easy. Please note: Do not use commercial sour cream. Let a cup of fresh heavy cream sit out until it sours. (I usually leave it out overnight.)

1   *cup soured cream (see comment above)*
1   *cup granulated sugar*
3   *eggs*
¾   *cup raisins*
1   *cup coarsely chopped walnut meats*
1   *teaspoon cinnamon*
1   *teaspoon allspice*
½   *teaspoon ground cloves*
1   *9-inch pie pan lined with unbaked pie pastry or graham cracker crust*

Stir soured cream and sugar together. Add slightly beaten eggs and blend well together. Add remaining ingredients and stir together. Put into un-baked pie shell. Bake in a moderate (350° F.) oven about 35 minutes or until knife blade inserted in center comes out clean.

QUEEN OF HEARTS TARTS

My mother was born in Idaho, out on Era Flat. She was a little tomboy, playing outside from dawn until dark, loving a tough old cat named Sabrina and a doll made out of a salt sack. Her mother made tartlets for her then, and called them QUEEN OF HEARTS TARTS. When my grandfather was away, they ate together in front of the wood stove and had supper of soup and bread—and QUEEN OF HEARTS TARTS. I've found that they are dear to little boy hearts, too.

> *plain pie pastry—enough for two 2-crust pies*
> *tart jelly*
> *sugar*

Make pie pastry. Roll out about ¼-inch thick. Cut into rounds (I use a jar lid), and from half the rounds remove centers (I use a whisky shot-glass). Brush plain rounds with cold water and press cut-out rounds on top. Bake in a hot (400° F.) oven until lightly browned. Press down centers gently while still warm. Sprinkle with sugar. Cool. Fill centers with a tart jelly.

FRONTIER PUDDINGS AND CANDY

Cooking on a wood range is no simple thing. The work starts with the wood fuel, with felling the tree and hauling it and cutting it into lengths—longer for the heat stove and shorter for the cook stove—and then splitting the lengths into stove wood, again larger for the heat stove and smaller for the cook stove. Then it is piled, and then it is hauled indoors in endless trips that get wood chips and dirt on your clean floor. Then a fire is started in the dratted stove, which is a frustratingly long procedure on frigid winter mornings when you are cold and want to hurry, and *then* you must keep adding wood at properly spaced intervals to keep the fire burning steadily because that is the only way you'll have an even temperature. I count as one of my major accomplishments the fact that I have built a fire on a winter morning at twenty below, and baked seven loaves of bread in one day. I fully intend to tell my grandchildren all about it.

The double-damned wood stove is only one reason why frontier desserts were often simple. The paucity of ingredients was another. These old-time desserts were easy to make from ingredients on hand. They were good then, and they are good now.

BREAD PUDDING
(SERVES FOUR)

2 *cups stale, torn bread*
3 *cups scalded milk*
1 *cup sugar*
1 *cup melted butter or margarine*
2 *eggs, slightly beaten*
½ *teaspoon salt*
1 *teaspoon vanilla or ¼ teaspoon cinnamon*

Soak torn bread in milk and set aside to cool. Add sugar, butter, eggs, salt, and vanilla or cinnamon. Stir and pour into a buttered 9″ × 9″ baking dish. Bake 1 hour at 325° F.

This good dessert is one that does well with imaginative additions such as ½ cup shredded coconut . . . ½ cup chocolate sauce or a small can of pitted sour cherries, sweetened to taste and thickened with cornstarch, swirled through before baking . . . ½ cup raisins . . . or ½ cup raisins and ½ cup chopped nuts.

CORNSTARCH PUDDING
(SERVES FOUR)

6 *tablespoons cornstarch*
⅔ *cup granulated sugar*
½ *teaspoon salt*
½ *cup cold milk*
4 *cups scalded milk*
2 *teaspoons vanilla*
  cinnamon

Mix cornstarch with sugar and salt. Add cold milk and stir until smooth, then pour mixture slowly into scalded milk, stirring constantly. Cook 15 minutes in a double boiler at a slow boil, stirring constantly until mixture thickens, and stirring occasionally during the remainder of cooking time. Cool slightly and add vanilla. Pour into bowls and sprinkle cinnamon on top. Chill.

POOR MAN'S PUDDING
(SERVES FOUR)

4   *cups milk*
¼   *cup unprocessed rice*
½   *cup raisins*
½   *teaspoon salt*
⅓   *cup molasses*
½   *teaspoon cinnamon*
2   *tablespoons butter or margarine*

Mix together all ingredients except butter and pour into a buttered baking dish. Bake at 300° F. for 3 hours, stirring several times during the first hour to keep the rice from settling to the bottom. At the last stirring, add the butter.

PIONEER CABIN-KITCHEN CANDY

One by one the old-timers of the West are going, and one by one they are gone. They were born before 1900 became a date, and time is running out for them. The West will not be the same when none are left.

They had great strengths. People left everything they had, everything that was familiar, to go to an unknown land and do what had not been done before. It must have been hard to leave behind the treasured possessions, and the familiar look of the land; to say good-bye forever to family and friends; and to turn their faces to the great distances and challenges before them.

Men built life and living and the places in which to do it all. Women had a courage that commands respect. One of my great-grandmothers came west as a young woman, and watched her baby die on the journey. She had to leave that tiny grave out on the lonely prairie and go on, looking back until the little headstone was out of sight—but no one saw her falter until I was born, when she was an old lady. My mother told me that when they put me in that old woman's arms, she put her face against my head and wept—and it was the first time anyone knew her tears.

These people gently closed the door on memories, and found laughter and moments of tenderness. They gathered in cabin kitchens that spilled golden light of candles and coal-oil lamps, and told stories and made candy and built new memories.

VINEGAR CANDY

2 *tablespoons butter or margarine*
2 *cups sugar*
½ *cup vinegar*
½ *teaspoon vanilla*

Melt margarine in heavy pan and add sugar and vinegar. Stir until sugar is dissolved, washing down the sides of the pan with a pastry brush dipped in cold water. Boil until mixture is brittle when dripped into cold water. Turn into a buttered flat pan and fold toward center as the mixture cools around the edges. Add vanilla as you work the candy. When cool enough to handle, grease fingers with butter, pick up chunks of candy, and pull and stretch until it is light-colored and porous. Cut in pieces with kitchen shears.

PEANUT BRITTLE

1½   cups granulated sugar
½   cup water
½   cup light corn syrup
1   cup coarsely chopped peanuts
1   tablespoon butter
1½   teaspoons baking soda

In a large saucepan mix sugar, water, and syrup. Bring to a boil, stirring constantly. Wash down the sides of the pan with a pastry brush dipped in cold water. Cook rapidly to the soft-crack stage (270° F.). Add nuts and continue cooking, stirring steadily, to the hard-crack stage (310° F.). Add remaining ingredients. As you stir, the candy will foam up—but don't be frightened. Pour into a buttered cookie sheet. When cold, break into pieces.

Chapter 10

HOMEMADE BREAD FOR PENNIES A LOAF

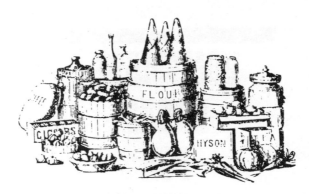

If you have never baked your own bread, try it at least once. The smell alone is worth the effort. The taste is full and slightly tangy, and the texture is both coarser and heavier than that of store-bought bread.

A loaf of homemade bread costs only about half as much as a bakery loaf—and that takes into consideration the escalated prices of sugar and flour, and figures in the cost of fuel to operate the oven. Use an inexpensive flour—the bread won't know the difference, but your budget will.

Making bread isn't a mysterious procedure. My first two loaves were pitiful, undernourished things, so flat and inadequate that we had to slice them horizontally (the long way) rather than with the normal vertical cut in order to have a slice big enough for a sandwich. The loaves were about 2½ inches high. The second time I tried, I kneaded the dough instead of dabbling delicately with it, and produced an honest loaf.

The first time or two that you make your own bread, the kneading process will seem mournfully weary; but after you get over the bashful stage, it is rather fun and you can work out any repressed angers you might be carrying around. Pound the dough and slap it, muttering "take that, and that and that and that," and both you and the bread will be better for it.

I use store-bought bread for sandwiches; and serve homemade bread with dinner or for breakfast toast. (I always make the equivalent of two loaves into rolls with which to stretch dinners.) Since I bake a lot of bread, I buy yeast in a large can as it is considerably cheaper that way; but you might want to start by buying a small jar or individual packets. Dry yeast is much easier to use and keep than compressed yeast cakes; and if the day is chilly or if you are in a hurry, you can sneak in a little extra yeast to make the dough rise faster.

PLAIN WHITE BREAD

(MAKES 5 LOAVES, OR 3 LOAVES AND 2 DOZEN ROLLS)

3   *tablespoons dry yeast or 3 packets*
1   *cup warm water*
⅓   *cup sugar*
3   *tablespoons salt*
⅓   *cup melted lard or shortening*
5   *cups lukewarm water*
14   *to 18 cups all-purpose flour*

Sprinkle yeast (plus an extra pinch if the day is cold) over 1 cup warm water. Combine sugar, salt, melted lard, and 5 cups lukewarm water in a very large bowl. Stir to blend. Sift in about 6 cups flour and stir together. (A wooden spoon works best and is easier on your hand.) Add yeast mixture and enough flour to make a stiff dough that cleans the bowl as you stir—about 8 to 10 cups, depending on the flour you use, but don't add it all at once. At some point in this step, the dough will be hard to stir and you will abandon the spoon and get your hands into it. Flour your hands first.

Turn dough out on a floured board and knead it for 5 minutes. Don't cheat.

If you aren't sure what "kneading" is (I wasn't), it means to fold the dough toward you with a rolling motion, using the fingers of both hands to pull it. With the heels of your hands press down and push the dough away from you. Turn the dough one-quarter turn and repeat the process. Keep going 5 minutes, or until the dough is smooth, satiny, and elastic. After you've kneaded dough a few times, you will know when it has been kneaded enough by the way it feels.

Place the kneaded dough in a large, well-greased bowl, then turn the dough over so that the greased side is up. Cover with a clean cloth or towel and let rise in a warm place until it has doubled in bulk—about 1½ hours. Poke a finger into the dough and if the hole your finger makes stays there, the dough is probably right.

Punch the dough down—be gentle, not angry—and turn it out onto a board again. Pull off roughly ⅔ of the dough and shape it into 3 loaves in greased bread pans. (Fill the pans about half full.) If there is a seam in your loaves, put that side down. Dab bits of butter over the tops of the loaves, cover with a clean cloth, and let rise until doubled again—about 1 hour. Shape the remaining dough into rolls, remembering that they will double in size. Make the rolls half the size you want the finished product to be—the size of an egg is about right for dinner rolls, double that for hamburger buns. Put the rolls in greased flat pans or cookie sheets and turn over so greased sides are up. (You can use shortening or lard.) Cover with a cloth and let rise until doubled—about 1 hour.

Bake the loaves and rolls in a hot (400° F.) oven for 15 minutes, then reduce heat to about 375° F. and bake 30 minutes. (If you bake bread in glass loaf pans, reduce the oven temperature by 25 degrees.) The bread is done when it responds with a hollow sound when you tap it. Immediately turn the loaves and rolls out on racks to cool, for if you don't your bread will be soggy. If you like crusty bread, let the loaves cool uncovered—but if you like a softer crust, put a dish towel over the loaves as they cool.

If you have trouble with holes in your bread that resemble those in Swiss cheese, eliminate them by pricking each loaf with a fork after you have put the dough in the bread pans and before the second rising.

It is not possible to slice hot bread neatly, but a loaf hot from the oven, torn into chunks and buttered, is a treat I haven't enough willpower to decline.

FRIED DOUGH

In pioneer days—and sometimes even today—fried dough cakes were called "dough gods." It isn't a bad name.

Fried dough can be a breakfast bread, a noontime sandwich base, a dinner hot roll substitute, or dessert at any time with syrup, honey, jelly, or powdered sugar sprinkled over. I have made it in pack-in camps miles deep in the Idaho wilderness, in a homestead cabin seventy miles from the nearest road, on a wild piece of British Columbian coast, and in my home kitchen to serve to city-bred guests. There was never a time I made it that guests did not ask for more and beg the recipe. It is so easy that it seems as if it can't be that good, but it is. This recipe is as old as the West itself.

When you bake bread, reserve the dough for one loaf. After you have put your remaining loaves and rolls to their second rising, just return the reserved portion to a bowl and cover it.

If you want fried bread when you are not planning to bake loaves, the following recipe will make a quantity of fried dough bread for four to six people: Sprinkle 1 tablespoon or 1 packet dry yeast over ¼ cup luke-warm water. Combine 2 tablespoons sugar, 1 tablespoon salt, and 2 tablespoons melted shortening or lard with 1½ cups lukewarm water. Stir in 4 to 5 cups flour. Knead and let rise as if for ordinary bread.

Just before you serve dinner, heat a heavy skillet. Add about ¼ cup of lard or cooking oil, or enough to cover the bottom of the skillet about ¼-inch deep. When it is hot but not smoking, drop in pieces of dough. (Prepare them while the oil is heating. Just pinch off a golf-ball-sized chunk of dough and spread it with your fingers, turning it as you work, until you have a pancake about ¼-inch thick. If the pancake is thicker than that, the dough won't cook through.)

Place the dough pancakes gently in the hot oil. Let them cook until the edges are golden, then gently turn them with a fork and cook the other side. They should be crispy on the outside and tender-soft in the middle.

Serve with butter and jelly, honey, syrup, or powdered sugar. Cold, sliced, and buttered, with meat in the middle, they are marvelous for back-pack sandwiches. They are hearty and filling and unreasonably good.

If you happen to be in Montana in July, during the American Indian Days celebration in the Blackfeet Reservation town of Browning, you will find stalls selling fried dough scattered all over the pow-wow grounds.

WHOLE WHEAT BREAD

The recipe for WHOLE WHEAT BREAD is very simple. Just use the recipe for PLAIN WHITE BREAD, but substitute whole wheat flour for half of the white flour. Everything else is the same.

HONEY WHOLE WHEAT BREAD
(MAKES THREE LOAVES)

I found this bread at a county fair in Montana, at a booth manned (or womaned) by a tall, curvy girl with long blond hair. She was lovely and gentle, and her bread is good.

½   *cup warm water*
2   *tablespoons or 2 packets dry yeast*
6   *tablespoons lard or other shortening*
¼   *cup honey*
4½   *cups water*
4   *cups whole wheat flour*
1   *cup mashed potatoes (2 medium potatoes, cooked) or ½ cup instant potato flakes, ½ cup instant dry milk, and 1 tablespoon salt*
6   *to 8 cups white all-purpose flour*

Combine warm water with yeast in a large bowl. Stir to dissolve yeast. Melt lard in a 6-quart saucepan. Remove from heat and add honey and water. Mix the whole wheat flour with the mashed potatoes or potato flakes and add to saucepan. Beat until smooth. Add yeast mixture and beat until smooth. With a wooden spoon, mix in enough white flour to make a dough that cleans the bowl as you stir—6 to 8 cups.

Turn out onto a lightly floured board and knead until smooth and satiny, and small blisters appear—probably 8 to 10 minutes. Place in a greased bowl and turn so the top is greased. Cover and let rise in a warm place until doubled—1 to 1½ hours. Punch down dough, divide into thirds, cover, and let rest a few minutes. Shape into 3 loaves and place in greased 9″ × 5″ × 2″ pans. Brush with melted butter, cover, and let rise until doubled—about 1 hour. Bake in a hot (400° F.) oven for about 45 minutes. Remove from pans and cool on racks.

TWO IRISH BREADS

The following two recipes—for IRISH FRECKLE BREAD and IRISH SODA BREAD—came west from Ireland to New York and then further west from New York to San Francisco. There are sons of *the auld sod* wearing policeman blue in the city by the Golden Gate as well as in the big city of Broadway. In San Francisco the names Sullivan, O'Grady, Kelly, and Murphy mingle with names like Paladini, Nakamura, Sing Lee, and Tarantino. My grandmother's name was Hanna and my husband's name is McBride, so Irish bread comes naturally to our house.

IRISH FRECKLE BREAD

(MAKES 4 LOAVES)

2   *tablespoons or 2 packets dry yeast*
1   *cup warm water*
¼   *cup lukewarm mashed potatoes (1 medium potato)*
8   *tablespoons sugar*
5   *cups all-purpose flour*
1   *teaspoon salt*
2   *eggs, beaten*
½   *cup melted margarine, cooled*
1   *cup seedless raisins*

Sprinkle yeast into warm water. Stir until dissolved. Add mashed potatoes, 2 tablespoons sugar, and 1 cup flour. Beat until smooth. Cover, and let rise in a warm place until bubbly—about 1 hour. Stir down. Add 6 tablespoons sugar, salt, and 1 cup flour. Beat until smooth. Stir in eggs, then margarine. Add raisins. Stir in enough additional flour to make a soft dough—2 to 3 cups. Turn out onto a lightly floured board and knead until smooth and elastic—about 5 minutes. Place in a greased bowl, turning the dough so the greased portion is on top. Cover and let rise until doubled—about 1 hour. Punch down and turn out onto a floured board. Divide into 4 equal parts. Let rest 5 minutes. Form each part into a smooth, round loaf and place in greased, deep pie dishes or on a greased cookie sheet. Cover and let rise in a warm place until doubled in bulk—about 45 minutes. Bake in a 350° F. oven about 25 minutes, or until done.

IRISH SODA BREAD
(MAKES 1 LOAF)

Baking powder is used instead of yeast in this recipe, and the kneading process is reduced accordingly.

4	*cups sifted all-purpose flour*
1/4	*cup sugar*
1	*teaspoon salt*
1	*teaspoon baking powder*
1	*teaspoon baking soda*
2	*tablespoons caraway seeds*
1/4	*cup butter or margarine*
2	*cups seedless raisins*
1 1/3	*cups buttermilk*
1	*egg*
1	*egg yolk*

Sift together flour, sugar, salt, baking powder, and baking soda. Stir in caraway seeds. Cut in butter until it is like coarse meal. Stir in raisins. Combine buttermilk with 1 egg and stir into flour mixture until it is just moistened. Turn dough out onto a lightly floured board and knead lightly until smooth. Shape into a loaf and put in a greased, 2-quart casserole dish. Cut a cross in the top about 1/2-inch deep. Brush top with a beaten egg yolk. Bake at 375° F. for about 1 hour to 1 1/4 hours, or until done when tested with a toothpick. Cool on a wire rack.

UNLEAVENED BREAD

For a good and unusual accompaniment to soups, stews, beans, and dips, and a good picnic and camp food, make unleavened bread. It is easy, and a great quantity of it costs only pennies. "Crackers" of unleavened bread are favorites in our house, served with the platters of fruit and cheese my family considers the best of all possible snacks.

5   cups all-purpose flour
1   tablespoon sugar
1   tablespoon salt
    water

Mix flour with sugar and salt. Add only enough water to make a stiff dough. Knead and pull it firmly (it will resist!) until the dough is smooth. Roll it out on a lightly floured board until dough is as thin as a soda cracker. Score it along the lines at which you will want it to break—squares, oblongs, and triangles. Bake on 12″ × 12″ cookie sheets at 350° F. for about 10 minutes, or until very lightly browned.

ONION BREAD

(MAKES 3 LOAVES)

The big cattle ranches of the West are small communities in themselves. Far-spaced, with many miles between neighbors, they have to be largely self-sufficient. Hospitality is a way of life—casual callers are always offered food and drink, and a warm, smiling welcome is typical. I remember so many ranch kitchens, where the social life is centered, for their fried ham and country scrambled eggs, salty jokes and laughter, and the smell of bread like this.

¾   cup milk
1   envelope onion soup mix
½   cup sugar
½   cup butter or margarine
2½   tablespoons or 2½ packets dry yeast
½   cup warm water
1   egg, beaten
4   cups all-purpose flour

Scald milk. Stir in onion soup mix and blend well. Stir in sugar and butter. Mix until butter melts. Cool to lukewarm. Sprinkle yeast over warm water and stir to dissolve. Add milk mixture, egg, and half the flour. Beat until smooth. Add remaining flour to make a stiff batter. Cover tightly and chill at least 2 hours. Put into 3 small, well-greased loaf pans, and brush with melted butter. Cover with a clean towel and let rise in a warm place until doubled in bulk. Bake at 375° F. for about 35 minutes, or until done. Remove from pans and brush again with melted butter.

DINNER ROLLS
(MAKES 24 ROLLS)

1	tablespoon or 1 packet dry yeast
1	cup lukewarm potato water (the water drained from boiled potatoes)
¼	cup sugar
2	teaspoons salt
6	tablespoons melted butter or margarine
2	eggs, beaten
3½	cups all-purpose flour, approximately

Dissolve yeast in potato water. Add sugar and salt and let stand 1 hour. Beat in melted butter and beaten eggs. Add about 3½ cups flour and knead until smooth and satiny—about 5 minutes. Let rise until doubled. Shape into rolls and let rise again until doubled. Bake at 400° F. for 25 minutes.

SUNDAY ROLLS
(MAKES 24 TO 30 ROLLS)

These delicate rolls are more than just delicious—they're also so easy to make that they will be among your favorite recipes. I know Sunday Rolls were made by my family forebears in Idaho in 1896.

2	cups scalded milk
½	cup butter or margarine
¼	cup sugar
1	teaspoon salt
1	yeast cake or 1 packet dry yeast
2	eggs, well beaten
3	to 4 cups flour

Scald milk, and add butter, sugar, and salt. Cool to lukewarm. Add yeast. When yeast has dissolved, stir in eggs and flour. Beat well. Cover, let rise until doubled—about 1½ hours. Fill buttered muffin pans about ⅔ full. Let rise until pans are full—about 1 hour. Bake 10 minutes in hot (400° F.) oven.

SOURDOUGH AND HOOCH

Sourdough is enjoying a new surge of popularity, especially among the simplicity-seekers of the new American culture, with sourdough crocks bubbling faithfully in kitchens all over the country. The art of sourdough cookery was never lost, for Western cooks scattered throughout the land have continued to use sourdough as it was used in pioneer days. My sourdough cookery is exactly the same as my grandfather's of seventy years ago.

The old cowboy and his prospecting counterpart in Alaska knew that the sourdough crock was the source of breakfast, lunch, dinner, dessert, and probably a dozen more uses, depending on the application of the sourdough jug to the problem at hand.

Sourdough makes superlative pancakes and waffles; unbeatable biscuits; a filling, savory bread; muffins; cookies; and cake. In all cases, the basic sourdough is the same.

Here's how to do it:

THE CARE AND FEEDING OF A SOURDOUGH CROCK

1. You will need a crock with a loosely fitting lid. Any glass jar will do, although crockery will help hold the starter (sometimes called "sponge") at a consistent temperature. *Never* use a metal container, as the acids in the starter will not only corrode the metal and discolor the starter, but will also cause the starter to spoil. Glass or earthenware—that is the first law.

2. Put a cup of unsifted, all-purpose flour into the crock. Dissolve a healthy tablespoon or one packet of dry yeast (or a package of compressed yeast) in a cup of warm water. Add to the flour and mix well. Cover and store in a warm place overnight. A temperature of 75° F. will insure an enthusiastic starter. By morning the starter will be

covered with small bubbles and will yield a tangy odor when you lift the lid. Add another cup of flour and a cup of warm water, stir well, and leave alone for 24 hours. Now your starter is ready to use in any of the recipes that follow.

3. *Whenever you remove starter from the crock, add flour and water to the remaining starter to keep it going.* Never use all the starter. Always leave at least a ½ cup in the crock, and take care of the crock before proceeding with your recipe. Add a cup of flour and a cup of warm water to the starter in the crock, stir well to blend, and never fail to clean the sides of the crock with a knife or rubber spatula. If you don't, the sourdough drippings on the sides of the crock will harden to a cementlike substance. If any of it flaked into your starter and got into, say, biscuits, the unwary might bite down and break a tooth. The unbelievable hardness of sourdough dried on any substance gives credence to the story that early-day homemakers used the stuff for wallpaper paste.

4. If you do not use your sourdough every day, you must add an occasional cup of flour and cup of water to keep the starter alive and vigorous—about every other day will keep a starter in fine shape. If you find yourself accumulating quantities of starter, reduce your starter to one cup and throw the remainder away. This will keep your starter fresh.

5. If you find your use of sourdough consistently infrequent, put a cup or so of your starter in a glass jar with a lid and refrigerate it. It will keep for several months. The starter will separate and a clear liquid will come to the surface. This clear liquid is called "hooch," and Indians of long ago discovered that it is intoxicating. That's where the slang word "hooch" for whiskey came from. When you reactivate your refrigerated starter, put it back in your crock with the hooch, stir, and add a cup each of flour and warm water. Stir well again, cover, and leave in a warm place (75° F. to 80° F.) overnight. It should be enthusiastic and resurrected again in the morning.

6. *Never, never, never add anything to your starter crock but warm water and flour.* Not ever. Don't ever pour leftover batter back into the crock.

7. When you have a large amount of starter going—as when you plan a hotcake breakfast for a number of people and have added 3 or more cups of flour and an equivalent amount of water to get a goodly

amount of starter—remember to stir it down in the crock at least once during the day. It does keep the starter light, but the main reason is to keep the starter from getting so vigorous that it spills down the sides of the crock.

8. Remember that you can kill the starter by keeping it too hot as well as by storing it in too cold a place. Seventy-five degrees is about right.

On to sourdough recipes.

SOURDOUGH BREAD
(MAKES 2 LOAVES)

"Set" the starter the night before you bake bread by adding 2 cups flour and 2 cups warm water to the starter in the crock. Let starter ferment at least 8 hours, then scrape out all but about ½ cup into a large bowl. To the starter remaining in the crock add a cup each of flour and warm water, stir well, and put back to keep working for you.

To the starter in the bowl, which should be about 3 cups, add 4 cups all-purpose flour that has been sifted with 1 teaspoon salt, 2 tablespoons sugar, and ½ teaspoon baking soda. Stir into the starter with about 2 tablespoons melted fat. Mix as well as you can. Knead on a lightly floured board about one hundred times, or until the dough is smooth. Do not add too much flour—it may vary from 4 cups, depending on the brand of flour and on the thickness of your starter. Use just enough flour to work the dough. The dough should be somewhat "tacky" to the touch—more so than is ordinary bread dough. Divide in half. Half fill 2 greased loaf pans. Work the dough into the corners of the pans and smooth it. Grease the tops and set in a warm place until doubled in bulk. Bake 20 minutes in a hot (400° F.) oven, then reduce heat to 325° F. and continue baking about 35 minutes, or until the loaf shrinks slightly from the sides of the pan and gives a hollow thunk when you tap it. Turn out onto a rack and cover with a towel to cool.

HONEY-WHEAT BREAD
(MAKES 2 LOAVES)

Follow the recipe for SOURDOUGH BREAD, but substitute 2 cups whole wheat flour for 2 cups of white flour, and add ¼ cup honey to the mixture.

SOURDOUGH CORN BREAD
(MAKES 1 LOAF)

Mix 1 cup starter with 1½ cups milk (evaporated milk works best), 1½ cups yellow cornmeal, 2 tablespoons sugar, ½ teaspoon salt, ½ teaspoon baking soda, 2 beaten eggs, and ¼ cup melted butter or margarine. Mix together well and turn into a 10-inch greased, heavy frying pan and bake in a 400° F. oven for about 25 minutes, or until a toothpick inserted in the center comes out clean.

SOURDOUGH BISCUITS
(MAKES 12 TO 16 BISCUITS)

For dinner biscuits, "set" your starter at breakfast by adding 2 cups each flour and warm water to the starter in the crock. Stir well and let ferment all day.

To make the biscuits, mix about 2 cups starter with ½ cup milk, 1 tablespoon sugar, 1 teaspoon salt, 1 teaspoon baking soda, and 2 tablespoons melted fat, oil, or bacon drippings. If your starter is thin and runny, omit the milk. Blend well, then work in enough flour to make a soft dough—between 2½ and 4 cups, depending on how thick or thin the basic starter is. Knead lightly. Pinch off dough the size of golf balls and roll into biscuits. Place close together in a well-greased baking pan, and turn over so greased sides are on top. Let rise in a warm place for about 45 minutes, then bake in a moderate (375° F.) oven for 30 minutes, or until biscuits are golden on top and give a hollow thunk when you tap them. My best pan of sourdough biscuits were a good 3 inches high.

SOURDOUGH PANCAKES
(MAKES 12 TO 16 CAKES)

One lovely autumn in Idaho, my husband, Tom, and I were packing supplies for a two-week horse trip into a wild place for wildlife photographs when it occurred to me that sourdough pancakes would be a real treat in camp. Visions of golden flapjacks dripping with butter and honey—a rhapsody in gold to match the turning leaves—flitted through my head, and I poured a cup of starter into a pint canning jar, screwed the lid on firmly, wrapped the jar in a cloth, and stuck it in the pocket of my parka.

The jar of starter made the twenty-mile horseback trip in fine shape, but when we got to our camp I was in a quandry over how to keep the starter warm all night. Nights then were already cold, and our fire wouldn't last until morning. We would wake to a frigid tent—and a dead sourdough starter. I remembered hearing my grandfather tell about taking his sourdough jug to bed with him to keep it warm, so I happily tucked my glass jar of sourdough into my new down sleeping bag and fell asleep still thinking of golden sourdough hotcakes for breakfast.

I awoke around four in the brisk morning decidedly uncomfortable, with the feeling that I was sleeping in quantities of cold gravy.

I fumbled for a flashlight and directed the beam down into my sleeping bag, and found that the lid had worked off the jar and my highly enthusiastic sourdough starter had fermented all over me, my clothing, and the inside of my new down sleeping bag. I spent what was left of the night —and well into the next day—scraping sourdough off everything to the unsympathetic comments of my husband. We didn't have sourdough hotcakes for breakfast, but parts of my sleeping bag were permanently stiffened. The moral of this tale is: If you take sourdough starter on a pack trip, tie the lid on securely. (I've tried it since with excellent results.)

Sourdough pancakes are worth any effort. If you intend to have pancakes for breakfast, get ready for them while you are doing the dinner dishes the night before. For a good quantity of sourdough pancake batter, start by adding 2 cups each of flour and warm water to the starter in your crock and stir in well.

In the morning the batter will be covered with small bubbles and will smell fresh and tangy. Pour all but a cup of starter into a large bowl, and feed your remaining starter with equal parts of flour and warm water before you proceed with your pancakes.

Your batter bowl should be higher than it is wide, because the batter will foam up. To the starter in the bowl add 2 eggs, 2 teaspoons salt, 1 tablespoon sugar, and 2 tablespoons cooking oil, melted lard, shortening, or bacon drippings. Blend in ingredients and stir well. The batter will rise and foam. Fry on a lightly greased, hot griddle. If the batter is too thick, thin with a little milk. The correct batter is fairly thin.

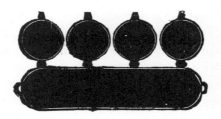

SOURDOUGH WAFFLES
(SERVES FOUR)

To make waffles, follow the same procedure as for pancakes, but add 2 additional tablespoons of oil and increase the heat of your waffle iron slightly beyond the ordinary waffle setting. For marvelous variations, either add ½ cup chopped nuts (pine nuts are superb!) to the batter before baking the waffles or lay strips of bacon across the waffle grid, close iron for 1 minute to slightly cook bacon, then open iron and pour batter over bacon. Reclose and bake waffle as usual.

SOURDOUGH TREATS AND DESSERTS

The basic sourdough starter will provide cookies and cakes in addition to breads, biscuits, and hotcakes. Try this recipe for an easy, inexpensive cookie that is also highly nutritious and a good keeper—if you can keep cookies long enough in your house to worry about freshness!

OATMEAL-GRANOLA COOKIES
(MAKES 40 TO 50 COOKIES)

1½	*cups brown sugar*
1	*cup shortening, or ½ cup shortening and ½ cup butter or margarine*
2	*cups sourdough starter*
2	*cups quick-cook oatmeal*
1	*cup granola*
1	*teaspoon cinnamon*
½	*teaspoon ground cloves*
½	*teaspoon nutmeg*
1	*teaspoon baking soda*
1½	*cups sifted flour*

Cream together brown sugar and shortening. Add starter, oatmeal, and granola. Sift cinnamon, cloves, nutmeg and baking soda with sifted flour and mix well into sourdough mixture. Chill 30 minutes, then roll out on a floured board and cut with a cookie cutter. Bake on a greased cookie sheet at 350° F. for about 15 minutes.

SOURDOUGH CHOCOLATE CAKE

The night before you bake this cake, add 1 cup all-purpose flour and ¾ cup warm water to your sourdough starter. The starter should be fairly thick.

1	cup sugar
½	cup shortening
2	eggs
1	cup thick sourdough starter
1	cup milk (evaporated works well)
1	teaspoon vanilla
3	squares melted semi-sweet chocolate
2	cups all-purpose flour
½	teaspoon salt
1½	teaspoons baking soda
1	teaspoon cinnamon

Cream together sugar and shortening. Add eggs and stir well. Add starter, milk, vanilla, and melted chocolate. Beat thoroughly for 2 minutes. Sift flour with salt, baking soda, and cinnamon and blend into sourdough mixture. Pour into greased and lightly floured cake pans and bake at 350° F. about 35 minutes. Use an 8″ × 8″ × 2″ square pan or two 8-inch round pans. Reduce baking time about 5 minutes if you use round pans. Frost with any topping you like on chocolate cake.

SOURDOUGH FRUIT CAKE

(MAKES SIX ONE-POUND LOAVES)

Sourdough Fruit Cake was a Christmas tradition for Western pioneers; and this recipe, adapted from early-day quantities, measurements, and supplies, makes as good a treat for today's families as it did for yesterday's.

1½	*cups light raisins*
1½	*cups dark raisins*
3	*cups mixed candied fruits and peels, or 3 cups of your own favorite blend*
½	*cup brandy*
½	*cup cider*
1	*cup granulated sugar*
1	*cup brown sugar, packed*
⅔	*cup shortening, or half shortening and half butter*
1½	*teaspoons cinnamon*
1	*teaspoon nutmeg*
½	*teaspoon allspice*
2	*eggs, well beaten*
1	*cup sourdough starter*
1	*cup chopped walnuts*
4	*cups sifted flour*
1	*teaspoon baking soda*
2	*teaspoons salt*

Coarsely chop raisins and candied fruit. Combine with mixture of brandy and cider, cover, and let stand overnight. Cream together sugars, shortening, and spices until light. Beat in eggs. Stir in sourdough starter and combine with fruit mixture. Add nuts. Stir well. Sift flour, baking soda, and salt together and add to batter. Mix thoroughly. Turn into six 9″ × 5″ × 3″ loaf pans that have been greased, lined with brown paper, and greased again. Bake for 2 to 2½ hours in a slow (275° F.) oven. Cool on wire racks before removing paper. Wrap in foil and refrigerate before slicing.

Chapter 11

ENTERTAINING DOESN'T HAVE TO BREAK THE BANK— BACKYARD BARBECUES AND PICNICS

The best way to use the land is to love it. Treat outdoors as another room of your house, nicer and larger than the rest—bedroom or kitchen or living room or all those at once.

If outdoor cookery isn't possible or appealing, cook inside and dine outside now and then on serene summer evenings. We have set our table under cherry trees in bloom, on the fire escape of a city apartment, and on the screened front porch of an elderly house in a small town. One of the most elegant dinners in my memory was a candlelit affair in a penthouse patio overlooking San Francisco at dusk.

Cooking indoors for dinner outdoors requires a menu with a minimum of toting in and out. Hot dishes have to be the kind that will stay hot, and anything elaborate is unacceptable because it requires too much work.

One of my favorite outdoor menus with indoor preparation is TAMALE PIE served with a tossed green salad, hot hard rolls, and FRUIT PUNCH.

TAMALE PIE
(SERVES SIX TO EIGHT)

If you are going to serve dinner at six o'clock, you can stay out of the kitchen until four. Make the fruit punch and refrigerate it to get it icy. Assemble TAMALE PIE and pop it in the oven. (If you wash the single saucepan, knife, and spoon, which the preparation stage requires, your kitchen is completely clear of a pots-and-pans cleanup.) Wrap rolls in a foil package so you can tuck them into the oven with the tamale pie during the last 15 minutes that it cooks. Stir the pie now and then from the bottom. Set the table outside. Relax. Fifteen minutes before serving time, put the rolls in the oven and make the salad. Hand various items to various people to carry to the table.

This tamale pie is especially good because it doesn't have the thick layer of cornmeal that is part of other tamale pie recipes.

1	brick chili, or 1 1-pound can chili without beans
1	can bouillon, undiluted
2	eggs, beaten
1	8-oz. can tomato sauce
1	#303 can whole, ripe pitted olives
1	4-oz. can sliced mushrooms, with liquid
1	#303 can whole kernel corn
1½	cups yellow cornmeal
1	teaspoon salt
¼	teaspoon pepper
½	teaspoon chili powder
¼	teaspoon garlic powder
1	pint milk

Cut chili into pieces or empty canned chili into a large saucepan, and add soup. Simmer, stirring frequently and watching that it does not scorch, until chili and soup are blended. Mix remaining ingredients in a 4-quart ovenproof casserole dish, blending well as you go. Pour in chili-soup mixture and stir well. Mixture will be soupy. Bake in a moderate (350° F.) oven until done—45 minutes to an hour—stirring from the bottom occasionally until the mixture is set.

Cool and tangy FRUIT PUNCH goes well with this menu.

1   *3-oz. package lime gelatin*
1   *cup boiling water*
1   *quart pineapple juice*
    juice of 2 lemons
1   *small bottle 7-Up or ginger ale*
1   *quart cold water*

Dissolve gelatin in boiling water and add remaining ingredients except 7-Up. Chill. Add 7-Up and stir well just before serving.

PEPPER POTS
(SERVES FOUR TO EIGHT)

Idaho and Montana share the Bitterroot Mountains. Montana looks west to see them making lovely sunsets for hundreds of miles. Their crest is the Idaho-Montana state line, and they hold wilderness deep in their tangled heart. There are few highway routes across them, although traces of old Indian trails can still be followed on foot by those with rugged hearts and tough legs. While lingering over this simple summer supper, we have watched the sun set behind the Bitterroots, and understood why Montana is called the "big sky" country. (Bitterroot old-timers are touchy about spelling "Bitterroot" as one word. They prefer Bitter Root. I think Bitterroot is prettier to look at.)

Serve the PEPPER POTS with a molded salad, slices of raisin bread spread with cream cheese, and FRUIT COOLER.

8   green peppers
2   cups diced leftover meat—ham, roast beef, meatloaf, or chicken
     —or sautéed hamburger
2   cups cooked rice
¼   cup finely chopped parsley
¼   cup chopped peeled onion
1   #303 can tomatoes
1   teaspoon chili powder
1   tablespoon Worcestershire sauce
½   teaspoon basil
¼   teaspoon thyme
1   teaspoon salt
     grated Parmesan cheese

Cut tops off peppers and remove seeds and inner membranes. Parboil 10 minutes. Drain. Combine next 10 ingredients and blend. Stuff peppers with mixture. Sprinkle generously with Parmesan cheese. Place in baking dish (set peppers close together so they will stand up) and pour 1 cup water into bottom of pan. Bake at 350° F. for 35 minutes.

FRUIT COOLER

2   6-oz. cans frozen lemonade, thawed
1   6-oz. can frozen orange juice, thawed
1   quart pineapple juice
3   quarts cold water

Combine ingredients and stir well. Chill thoroughly.

LEGGY CHICKEN
(SERVES SIX)

Serve MEXICALI CORN BREAD, cabbage slaw, and lemonade with this easy outdoor dinner.

12   chicken legs (so everyone can have 2)
2   eggs, beaten
1½   cups cracker crumbs
1   teaspoon salt
½   teaspoon pepper
¼   teaspoon garlic powder
¼   teaspoon poultry seasoning
½   cup butter or margarine

Dip chicken legs first in egg, then in cracker crumbs. Place in greased baking dish. Blend seasonings and sprinkle over chicken. Dot with butter. Cover and bake at 350° F. for 45 minutes. Uncover and bake 15 minutes longer.

MEXICALI CORN BREAD

1   4-oz. can roasted and peeled green chilies
1   cup yellow cornmeal
1   cup all-purpose flour
4   teaspoons baking powder
1   teaspoon salt
¼   cup softened butter or margarine
1   cup milk
1   egg
2   cups shredded cheddar cheese
1   #303 can whole kernel corn, drained
1   pimento, chopped

Scrape seeds out of chilies. Cut chilies into fine bits. (They are hot.) Blend cornmeal, flour, baking powder, and salt. Add margarine, milk, and egg, and beat until smooth. Stir in remaining ingredients and blend well. Pour into a hot, greased 9-inch skillet and bake at 400° F. about 30 minutes. Serve while still hot.

TRADITIONAL OUTDOOR SALADS

If all the outdoor meals revolving around macaroni salad or potato salad were laid end-to-end, they would circle the moon. In the big-land "out West," the two salads are made the same way, with the only difference being that one is made with cooked macaroni and the other with boiled potatoes. The success secret is to assemble the salads while the macaroni or potatoes are still hot so that the flavors of the ingredients will be better absorbed. This is a difficult process with hot boiled potatoes; but if you hold them in a damp cloth while peeling and chopping, you can avoid burned fingers. (I think they cook up too pulpy if you peel or chop before cooking.)

To 6 large potatoes, boiled until tender then peeled and chopped, or 1 pound salad or elbow macaroni, cooked until just tender and drained well, add:

> 3   *large dill pickles, chopped finely*
> 3   *sweet pickles, chopped finely*
> 1   *onion peeled and chopped finely (red onions are best)*
> 1   *stalk celery, minced*
> 2   *hard-cooked eggs, chopped*
> ½   *green pepper, chopped finely (optional)*
> ¼   *cup syrup from sweet pickles*
>   *few drops of yellow food coloring (be careful!)*
>   *mayonnaise to moisten well*

Mix all ingredients together while potatoes or macaroni are still hot, blending well to distribute food coloring evenly. (Make a potato salad something to brag about by adding a can of well-drained shrimp.) Be generous with the mayonnaise because the hot ingredients will absorb it and the salad will be too dry if you are stingy. The yellow food coloring gives the salad color that makes it taste richer because it looks richer.

HAMBURGER HOP-ALONG

Now that a macaroni or potato salad is built, prepare HAMBURGER
HOP-ALONG for a super outdoor dinner, served on the grass as the day ends.
This recipe makes a formidable amount, for a purpose: What is left over
freezes or cans beautifully, or keeps in the refrigerator for several days. It
can be reheated at picnics; used in other recipes; and served hot for lunch
or dinner—over rice, noodles, mashed potatoes, or scrambled eggs, or into
parboiled green peppers.

7	*pounds hamburger*
6	*small onions, peeled and chopped*
3	*stalks celery, sliced*
½	*cup flour*
1	*pint ketchup*
1	*quart tomato juice*
½	*bottle A-1 sauce*
2	*teaspoon curry powder*
½	*teaspoon garlic powder*
3	*bay leaves*
	salt and pepper to taste

Brown hamburger with onion and celery. (Since there is a large quantity
of hamburger, brown a pound or 2 at a time.) Put in a large kettle. Sprinkle
with flour and stir well. Add remaining ingredients, bring to a fast simmer,
reduce heat, and simmer gently for 30 minutes. Remove bay leaves.

Ladle generously over split hamburger buns or hard rolls. Serve with
a well-chilled potato or macaroni salad and iced tea.

POOR BOYS
(SERVES FOUR TO SIX)

When the temperature simmers and summer is sticky, serve a cold supper
under a tree. Make a potato salad early in the day and refrigerate it. Make
the FRUIT DRINK at the same time so it will be icy-cold. Stay out of the

kitchen until just before dinner, when it is time to construct the POOR BOYS. Play hide-and-seek after dark, with the timeless call of "olly-olly-ox-in-free!" floating in the summer night.

1   *loaf sourdough French bread*
     herb butter (recipe follows)
4   *to 6 slices salami*
4   *to 6 slices Monterey Jack cheese*
4   *to 6 slices boiled ham*
1   *red onion, peeled and sliced*
3   *tablespoons dry mustard*
1   *tablespoon any wine*

Cut bread in half lengthwise. To make herb butter, soften ⅔ cup butter or margarine and blend well with ⅛ teaspoon each thyme and basil, and a pinch ground sage. Spread evenly on bottom half of loaf. Layer salami, cheese, boiled ham, and onions, overlapping slices on bottom half of loaf. Mix mustard with wine and blend well. Spread thinly on top half of loaf. Put loaf together and cut into 4 to 6 slices.

FRUIT DRINK

2   *packages unsweetened raspberry or cherry instant soft drink*
     mix
½   *cup sugar*
1   *6-oz. can frozen lemonade, thawed*
1½   *quarts apple juice*
2   *quarts cold water*
     toothpicks skewered alternately with maraschino cherries and
     pineapple tidbits

Combine first 5 ingredients with juice from the can of pineapple tidbits, which you used for the skewers. Stir well to dissolve sugar. Put a fruit-skewered toothpick in each tall glass. Cover with well-chilled fruit drink.

PATIO PARTY

Only one in my family has a birthday to celebrate during the summer months. When that one turned five, I delighted his little boy heart with this menu—climaxed with a cake decorated with five 4th-of-July sparklers instead of candles.

PARTY MELON

1   *ripe watermelon*
4   *tart apples, unpeeled, diced*
1   *large bunch seedless grapes*
4   *ripe peaches, peeled and chopped*
4   *ripe pears, peeled and chopped*
1   *cantaloupe, peeled and chopped*
1   *honeydew melon, peeled and chopped*
1   *#303 can pineapple chunks, or 2 cups fresh pineapple*
1   *cup shredded coconut*
1   *cup chopped nuts—any kind*
    juice of 1 lemon
1   *quart ginger ale*

A festive container can be made out of the watermelon, into which you will put the rest of the ingredients. Cut watermelon horizontally into 2 sections, about ⅔ up the melon. (If you have an artistic hand, cut with a sawtooth edge.) Carefully scoop out the flesh, discard seeds and cut into bite-sized chunks.

Put watermelon chunks into a very large bowl and add remaining ingredients except ginger ale. Sprinkle lemon juice over fruit. Cover bowl with foil or plastic wrap and chill both the larger watermelon shell and the bowl of fruit until serving time. A few minutes before serving, gently mix fruits together and, with the juices that have accumulated in the bowl, pour into the chilled watermelon shell. Pour cold ginger ale over the top. (Now is the time, for a delightful difference, to substitute champagne, Cold Duck, or a sparkling rosé wine for the ginger ale.)

With the imposing, fruit-filled watermelon, serve a plate of sliced cheeses and paper-thin slices of ham, arranged alternately in an overlapping circle, and a platter of thinly sliced dark rye, pumpernickel, and sourdough French breads.

PICNICS

Everybody loves a picnic—except, perhaps, mother, who has to make all the preparations.

As for me, I love picnics. But I don't work very hard on them. I have, in my time, competed in elaborate night-before endurance races in order to have a menu of cold fried chicken, potato salad, chocolate layer cake, potato chips and dip, and icy lemonade—but no more.

My favorite picnic menu is a traveler's smorgasbord. We often lunch on this while we're driving to a far place, too, for we enjoy it and it's easy to handle in a car.

Get a large assortment of cheeses. We like to include a sharp cheddar, a mild cheddar, a slightly salty cheese (such as a Norwegian graddost or a bleu cheese), smoky Swiss cheese, and a rich dessert-type (such as gjetost, that tastes like sweet, smoked cream).

Add dry Italian salami, and several cans of your favorite sardines. Two kinds of crackers go along—Norwegian flat bread is good for one of them, as well as a small loaf of party rye bread or San Francisco sourdough French bread. Add a stick of butter or margarine and a jar of spicy mustard. Have FREIGHTERS for dessert (see Chapter 12 for the recipe). Since you've done little or no cooking, you won't mind making a gallon jug full of lemonade. Take paper cups, paper plates, several knives, and a good cutting board. That's your picnic. It's casual and delicious, everybody serves himself, you can eat off and on all day without a great to-do, and there might be enough left over for snacking at home.

Sometimes we do get more elaborate, especially if we are picnicking in the middle of a Northwest winter when there is a considerable layer of snow on the ground and the temperature is thick with cold. Oh, yes—we picnic then, too.

In our family the birthday boy is "King for a Day," and gets to choose what he wants for dinner and where he wants to have it. It happens that our older son, Mark, who has a birthday in July, usually decides on something shattering such as broiled T-bones on the Middle Fork of the Salmon River

—his sixteenth birthday—or a steak fry at Two Jack Lake in Canada—his eighteenth.

T-Lee, our younger son, has his birthday on New Year's Eve. *He* wants an outdoor event, too—and we don't see why he should not have it. On his fifth birthday, we drove our van as far as we could up a snow-choked road called East Fork, at the northern end of Lost Trail Pass on the Idaho-Montana state line. We ate birthday dinner there, then snowshoed around on new Christmas snowshoes. Our menu was Cornish game hens stuffed with rice and mushrooms, homemade hot rolls with honey, and a birthday cake with yellow frosting and five brave candles.

On the day-before-birthday, I mixed 2 cups cooked rice with a cup of sliced fresh mushrooms, four sliced green onions, and 1 stalk celery thinly sliced, all of which had been lightly sautéed in oil. Then I mixed the rice and vegetables together with soy sauce to suit my taste (about 2 table-spoons) and ½ cup of coarsely chopped pecans, and stuffed the game hens with the mixture—one for each of us. Each hen was rubbed lavishly with butter, then wrapped in a generous sheet of foil. I put the hens in a roasting pan and roasted them at 300° F. for 2 hours, pushed down the foil so they would turn a nice golden brown, and roasted 20 minutes longer. When they cooled, I rewrapped the foil around them and refrigerated immediately.

I made rolls, and when they cooled I wrapped them in a package of foil—12 to the package for four of us. I baked and decorated the cake, and hid the birthday gifts in the back of the car with the portable camp stove and the picnic basket of dishes. At departure time next day, I put the game hens, still in their foil blankets, back in the roasting pan for traveling.

An hour before dinner, I lighted the camp stove and put the roasting pan on. It covered both burners, so I tucked the foil-packaged rolls on top of the hens. Then I carefully poured 1 cup of water around the hens and put the cover on the roasting pan. It took 40 minutes for the hens and stuffing to reheat thoroughly, and by that time the rolls were piping hot, too.

A can of honey to spread on the rolls was so cold it was too thick to spread, so it went on a burner to warm, while water came to a boil on the second burner to make tea for adults and hot chocolate out of instant mix for the children.

It was a memorable birthday dinner. Try it sometime.

ICE-FISHING STEW

Ice fishing is great fun. I don't know how it ranks as fishing with Bluenose fishermen, but as recreation it is tops with our family. The lakes are frozen and lovely, and laughter echoes across the ice. We always have dinner on the lakeshore.

If you have a portable camp stove to take along, make a stew the day before to warm up at shoreline. Tote the stew in the kettle it cooks in. Reheat the stew and serve with rolls to dunk, and make tea in a billycan. If you don't know what a billycan is—it's just a big cleaned tin can. An empty 3-pound coffee can makes a good one, and my best billycan is the same size can that once held honey. It has a wire bail.

Our favorite ice-fishing stew is one we shared with friends on a splendid ice-fishing day, when Wynn, the most dedicated fisherman we know, had to take second place to our older son, Mark, who landed a 6½-pound rainbow trout. Wynn is tall, dark, and sardonic, and his wry wit doubles me up with laughter. He also vacuums up food in great quantities and stays lean as a whip. He vacuumed this stew, grumbling all the while about impertinent nineteen-year-old boys who out-fish their elders.

In a large kettle put about 6 beef neck bones or an equal number of beef rib bones. Add 2 quarts water and bring to a boil. Reduce heat, cover kettle, and simmer 1 hour. Then add:

3	*medium potatoes, scrubbed but not peeled, cut in chunks*
2	*carrots, scrubbed but not scraped, sliced*
1	*#303 can tomatoes, mashed*
3	*stalks celery, sliced*
2	*large onions, peeled and chopped*
½	*cup pearl barley or rice*
	salt and pepper to taste
1	*bay leaf*

Simmer until vegetables are done. In addition to salt, pepper, and the bay leaf, I often add ½ teaspoon mixed Italian seasonings and ¼ teaspoon garlic powder. Serve in bowls, with a bone in each. Meat scraps come off when diners inelegantly gnaw the bones—and on ice-fishing trips, "manners" are much more casual than they are at home!

HOBOS

HOBOS are hearty sandwiches, wrapped in foil and taken on a trip. At picnic time, build a small fire. When it has burned down to coals, place Hobos on a grill over the coals. Heat for 10 minutes and turn occasionally. Serve with that potato salad you wanted to make, but for heaven's sake, be sure you have kept it well chilled—unless you want to risk making everyone terribly ill. You see, bacteria grow very rapidly in potato or macaroni salads unless they are kept cold. I'd much prefer to take raw vegetables—carrots, celery, green onions, and green peppers—and some fruit and cheese to accompany my Hobos.

You will need 1 crusty French roll for each Hobo. Slice in half. On one half spread butter or margarine. On the other half spread mustard thinly. Starting on the mustard half, layer sliced luncheon meat or cooked ham, sliced onion, sliced tomatoes, sliced American cheese, and a slice of crisp bacon. Top with the buttered half of the roll. Wrap snugly in foil.

YOHOS
(MAKES EIGHT SERVINGS)

We think the best picnics revolve around a campfire. An old oven grate is great for propping over coals as a cooking surface. The HOBOS we just told you about cook on them, and so do YOHO sandwiches, named after a lovely wild place at the toe of a glacier in British Columbia where I first made them.

2	*pounds hamburger*
1	*cup uncooked oatmeal*
1/4	*cup wheat germ*
1/2	*cup peeled chopped onion*
2	*teaspoons salt*
1/4	*teaspoon pepper*
	dash liquid smoke flavor (optional)
1	*cup tomato juice*

Mix all ingredients well and shape into 8 patties. Pan fry over low heat until meat is just browned, turn, and barely brown on the second side. Chill. Wrap each patty in foil and refrigerate until time to go picnicking. Place wrapped patties on grill and cook about 5 minutes on the first side, turn, and cook 2 minutes longer.

While patties are cooking, place 16 slices buttered sourdough bread in a snug foil wrapping and heat on the grill. Slip patties from foil onto a bread slice. Top with what you like—thinly sliced pickle, sliced tomato, or lettuce, or all of them—and cover with a second slice of heated French bread.

FOLDOVERS
(MAKES SIX GENEROUS SERVINGS)

FOLDOVERS take more at-home preparation time than most of my picnic menus so I make double and triple recipes and freeze them. Then they are ready to pack and tote whenever a picnic happens. Since the foil-wrapped, frozen Foldovers are cold, I tuck lettuce and makings for green salad around them to stay crisp on the way to a picnic spot. A summery drink and fruit finish the picnic in grand style.

1	cup milk
2	teaspoons sugar
1	teaspoon salt
1	tablespoon dry yeast or 1 packet
1/2	cup warm water
3	cups sifted white flour
1	cup sifted whole wheat flour
1 1/2	pounds hamburger
1/2	cup chopped peeled onion
1/4	cup chopped celery
2	teaspoons salt
1/4	teaspoon pepper
1/4	teaspoon garlic powder
1/8	teaspoon cumin
1	8-oz. can tomato sauce
1/2	cup shredded cheddar cheese
1/2	cup cooked rice

Scald milk. Stir in sugar and salt and cool to lukewarm. Dissolve yeast in warm water. Stir cooled milk mixture into yeast. Add flour and mix well. Turn out on a floured board and knead until elastic—about 5 minutes. Place in a greased bowl. Cover and let rise in a warm place until doubled— about 1 hour.

While dough is rising, brown hamburger, onion, and celery in a small amount of oil, stirring so hamburger will be crumbly. Pour off excess fat. Stir in remaining ingredients. Simmer gently 10 minutes.

When dough has doubled, roll out very thin on a floured board. Cut into 6 evenly sized squares. Divide beef mixture into 6 equal portions and put 1 portion in the middle of each dough square. Fold over as for turn-overs and seal edges with a fork.

Place on a lightly oiled baking sheet and let rise in a warm place 30 minutes. Make a small slit in the top of each Foldover. Bake at 350° F. for 20 minutes. Let cool.

Spread butter on each cooled Foldover, and wrap in foil. If you make large batches for future Foldovers, now is the time to freeze them.

At picnic time, put wrapped Foldovers on a grate and heat. Thawed Foldovers will take 5 minutes per side; frozen Foldovers will take closer to 20 minutes per side.

COOKING OUT

Food for picnics is usually prepared at home and is eaten as-is at the picnic or just reheated. Cookouts are different because the food is prepared outside. The cookout may be in your own backyard, on the banks of a river, at the beach, off somewhere in the woods, or on a one-day excursion to a nearby national park or public campground. The site is accessible by car because of the food involved and because it is a short-term affair. Cookouts are economical in all respects: the need for entertainment and table decor is eliminated; time spent in food preparation becomes part of the fun; menus are always simple; and you can be as extravagant or as frugal as you like on ingredients. At a cookout, hamburgers are just as appropriate as steak.

A good cookout depends on the cooking fire. You'll keep it small, because cooking fires should not warm half the world. I keep saying that oven grates are great, which is a bad pun but a good idea. Oven grates are a fine size to cook on, the metal is heat-tempered (which is not always the case with refrigerator shelving), and they take up next to no room in a car. Scoop out a shallow depression slightly smaller than the grate for the fire, arrange rocks around the edges, lay the grate on the rocks, and build a small, steady fire under it. Cook directly on the grate. Keep the fire more coals than blaze and you'll do better.

Another good cooking fire can be built in a hole. Dig a hole about 18 inches deep and 2 inches smaller all around than your grate. Build a fire in the hole—a good, hot fire—and keep it going until there is a bed of hot coals about 6 inches from the top. Then lay your grate over the hole and cook on it. You may have to tuck small sticks into the coals in one place or another to keep the coals hot. Fill the hole when you leave for home, completely covering fire traces, so that the charcoal and ashes can return to soil.

You can also make a terrific portable barbecue brazier out of a twenty-gallon metal drum. Cut the drum in half the long way. Fill the bottom with a 2-inch layer of coarse sand, lay a piece of heavy-gauged, tightly woven wire over the opening, and use charcoal briquets or wood chips for fuel under the wire.

If you build a fire on sand or dirt, please . . . cover it completely when you leave. Then you will know the fire is out and you will also have obliterated your traces. In the woods, don't ever build a fire in pine duff. Fire travels under it, burining without a trace until it erupts suddenly, hours or days later, into the incomprehensible horror of a forest fire. We've lived in and on the edges of wild places for so many years that just the thought of fire raging across ridges literally makes me ill.

A cookout menu usually revolves around one main dish actually cooked out. The rest of the menu is often raw vegetables and fruit. If other items are cooked out, they will usually be potatoes and/or corn roasted in the coals, and perhaps a special cookout bread.

To get coal-roasted corn and potatoes out of the way first, go about them like this:

ROASTED POTATOES

Select medium-sized potatoes. Remove a thin slice from one end to reduce the possibility of having potatoes explode in the coals and pelt everyone with blistering bits. Scrub, and rub generously with oil, bacon fat, or butter. Wrap in a double layer of heavy-gauged foil. Put in the coals, around the edges of the cooking fire. Turn several times.

Cooking time depends on the size of potatoes and the heat of the fire, so it is best to test for doneness by piercing with a long-handled fork. Forty-five minutes is an average time.

You can bake spuds in just their skins. In that case, put them in hot ashes, not glowing coals, and leave them until they pierce easily with a fork. Break them in half and sprinkle with salt and pepper and a generous lump of butter or margarine. Eat them right out of their fire-blackened shells.

ROASTED CORN ON THE COB

Pull husks back from ears of corn without removing them. Remove corn silk. Replace husks and tie in place with stout string. Soak corn in salted water for 5 minutes. Drain. Roast on a grill over a hot fire 10 minutes, turning frequently. Remove husks and serve with butter or margarine and salt. If you want to roast the corn in the coals, bury it among the hot coals for about 5 minutes. If the husks are scanty, wrap a double layer of foil snugly over the husks.

COOKOUT BREAD

This bread is, of course, applicable to picnics or dinners at home, too. I put it in this chapter because I use it often on cookouts. Prepare it at home and tote it to the camp-out for heating on the great grate.

Buy or bake a long loaf of French bread. Cut it into thick slices, cutting into but not through the bottom crust, as the intact bottom crust holds the slices together. Butter the slices on both sides. Nudge the buttered slices back together and wrap the loaf in foil. When dinner is almost ready, put the foil package on the grate and turn it every few minutes until bread is hot through.

FOUR SEASONED BUTTERS FOR HOT BREAD

GARLIC BUTTER

Soften 1 cup butter or margarine. Add 1 peeled and crushed clove garlic and 1 teaspoon minced parsley. Blend.

SMOKE BUTTER

Soften 1 cup butter or margarine. Add 1½ teaspoon liquid smoke and ½ teaspoon paprika. Blend.

TANGY BUTTER

Soften 1 cup butter or margarine. Add ⅓ cup crumbled bleu cheese. Blend.

ITALIANO BUTTER

Soften 1 cup butter or margarine. Add ½ teaspoon mixed Italian herbs or ⅛ teaspoon each oregano, marjoram, basil, and rosemary. Blend. Spread on slices and sprinkle with grated cheese.

STEAKS ARE SERIOUS

When you invest a sobering amount of money in a costly steak barbecue involving T-bone, club, rib, filet mignon, or porterhouse, you'd better be in a serious frame of mind.

You should grill any steak on a fire that has burned down to about a 4-inch bed of coals. Spread the coals out evenly, and call them ready for the steak when they are glowing—not blazing—and have on them a light covering of white ash. Bring the steak to room temperature and place it about six inches from the bed of coals. For 1½-inch steak, 5 minutes on each side will result in rare perfection; 6 minutes on each side will bring it to medium rare; and 10 minutes per side will take the meat to well-done. (Remember that meat will cook for a while from its own heat after you remove it from the coals.)

For a massive sirloin to be cut for a party of people, get a giant cut 3- to 3½-inches thick, put it over a bed of embers, and allow 30 minutes per side. Don't ever let the fire blaze up to touch the meat.

When the steaks are done to the degree you like, pour melted butter over them and serve.

STEAK SAUCES

If you are a sauce addict, you might try one of these tried-and-true marinades. Let the meat rest in the sauce for at least an hour—or overnight—and baste with the sauce while the steak is cooking.

SPICY SAUCE

Mix together ¼ cup vinegar, ¼ cup oil, 2 tablespoons finely minced peeled onion, 1 crushed clove garlic, and ½ teaspoon each salt, dry mustard, and sweet basil.

ARIZONA SAUCE

Stir together until well blended 1 cup ketchup; ½ cup each oil, vinegar, and water; 1 tablespoon each Worcestershire sauce and brown sugar; ½ cup minced peeled onion; ½ teaspoon each salt, garlic powder, oregano; ¼ teaspoon ground cloves; 1 teaspoon chili powder; 1 crushed bay leaf. Heat over medium heat, stirring frequently, and simmer for 15 minutes. Cool before using.

BRUSH-ON SAUCE

Blend together 4 cloves garlic, mashed; 1 tablespoon salt; 2 tablespoons lemon juice; 1 teaspoon soy sauce; ⅓ cup oil. Brush on steaks while they are broiling.

MULTIPLE-USE SAUCE

This sauce goes on everything. Barbecue halved chickens, steaks, spareribs, short ribs, or even frankfurters in the same sauce.

1	8-oz. can tomato sauce
¼	cup vinegar
¼	cup oil
¼	teaspoon sweet basil
1	cup brown sugar, packed
2	cloves garlic, crushed
1	teaspoon rosemary

Combine ingredients and stir together until sugar is dissolved and sauce is smooth. Pour half over meat. Use the remainder to baste with while meat is cooking.

COOKOUT CHICKEN

As a sauce for cookout chicken, use either the MULTIPLE-USE SAUCE previously described or one of the two following recipes. The MULTIPLE-USE SAUCE is sweeter, the CALIFORNIA SAUCE is saltier and the MIDWAY SAUCE is a compromise.

Split broiler chickens in halves or quarters. Brush with sauce or pour sauce in a shallow pan and lay chickens in sauce. Let chicken rest for about an hour and turn occasionally or rebrush with sauce. Place on grill, hollow side down, when the coals are whitened with ash. Brush chicken often with sauce, and turn every 10 minutes. Figure 20 to 25 minutes for each side. Test chicken for doneness by wriggling one leg. If it gives easily, the chicken is done.

CHICKEN SAUCES
CALIFORNIA SAUCE

Combine 1 cup oil; ½ cup soy sauce; 3 cloves garlic, crushed; and 1 teaspoon oregano.

MIDWAY SAUCE

Combine in a jar with a tightly fitting lid ¾ cup oil; ¼ cup melted butter or margarine; ¼ cup lemon juice; 1 tablespoon dry mustard; 2 tablespoons brown sugar; 1 tablespoon salt; 1 teaspoon rosemary; ½ teaspoon pepper; 1 tablespoon grated onion; 1 clove garlic, crushed; 1 teaspoon Worcestershire sauce; ⅓ cup ketchup; dash tabasco sauce. Let stand overnight. Shake well before using.

GRILLED HAM

For a change of taste and pace, try grilling ham slices outside. Slice ham about ½-inch thick. When the coals are white, place heavy foil on top of the grill. Lay the ham slices on the foil and cook for 15 minutes. Turn slices over and brush generously with sauce. Cook about 15 minutes, brushing frequently with sauce. Pork chops can be used in place of ham, but they must cook about twice as long.

HAM SAUCES

BASIC HAM SAUCE

Mix ½ cup honey with ½ cup brown sugar; 2 tablespoons flour; 1 teaspoon dry mustard; and 3 tablespoons pineapple juice.

HAM SAUCE ELEGANT

Marinate ham slices overnight in this sauce. Broil for 10 minutes on each side when the coals are white, basting frequently.

Combine 2 cups sherry and ¼ cup melted butter or margarine; 3 tablespoons dry mustard; ¼ cup brown sugar; ¼ teaspoon garlic powder; ½ teaspoon rosemary; ½ teaspoon paprika; and ¼ teaspoon thyme.

HAMBURGERS ARE TRADITIONAL

Hamburgers grilled outdoors at a cookout are as traditional as bells at Christmas. Here are two of our favorite ways of going about preparing them.

BEACHBURGERS
(FOR SIX HAMBURGERS)

1	*teaspoon salt*
¼	*teaspoon pepper*
1	*tablespoon prepared mustard*
½	*cup finely chopped peeled onion*
¼	*cup pickle relish*
1½	*pounds ground beef*

Blend first 5 ingredients with ground beef and shape into 6 patties. Grill for 10 minutes, when the coals are white. Turn carefully and continue grilling until meat is done to your liking. Slip into a warmed hamburger bun and decorate with your favorite hamburger dressings.

SUPER BURGERS

For super hamburgers, making a hamburger each for five people, you'll need:

2	*pounds ground beef*
1	*onion, peeled and sliced thinly*
	ketchup
1	*cup American cheese, cut into ½-inch cubes*
	salt and pepper
1	*tablespoon prepared mustard blended with 2 tablespoons mayonnaise*
	pickle relish

Divide ground beef into 10 portions. Flatten into patties about 4 inches across and ½-inch thick. Spread 5 of the patties with ketchup to within ¼ inch of the edge. Season with salt and pepper. Gently spread 1 teaspoon pickle relish on top of ketchup. Top with a sprinkle of cheese cubes and an onion slice. Spread the remaining patties with the blended mustard and mayonnaise. Lay on the built-up patties, spread side down. Seal edges together. Butter completely the outside of the double patties. Grill over whitened coals for 10 minutes. Turn and continue grilling until meat is cooked to the degree you like. Slip into heated buns.

SPIRAL HOT DOGS

Hot dogs are not frequently served in our house because I'm not comfortable about the additives and ingredients that go into them. Now and then I find what I consider *good* frankfurters, and we have a cookout featuring these spirals.

Heat hot dog buns in a foil package. Slit frankfurters lengthwise and spread insides with mustard or ketchup or both. Insert a slice of dill pickle and a few bits of chopped onion. Wrap frankfurters in a spiral of a bacon slice and close with toothpicks. Broil over embers until bacon is crisp. Butter heated hot dog buns or spread with mayonnaise, and insert hot dogs. Remove toothpicks first!

SHISH KABOBS

Shish kabob started out in Turkey and it was originally made only of lamb or mutton. It traveled west to Greece, and then crept onward and branched out to include beef. It also became my favorite cookout feature.

TRADITIONAL LAMB KABOBS
(SERVES FOUR)

1½	pounds lamb shoulder, cut into 1-inch cubes
⅔	cup oil
½	cup lemon juice
2	teaspoons salt
½	teaspoon pepper
¼	teaspoon thyme
¼	cup ketchup
1	clove garlic, crushed
½	pound fresh mushrooms
2	onions, peeled and cut into quarters
2	tomatoes cut into wedges
2	green peppers cut into chunks

Combine oil, lemon juice, salt, pepper, thyme, ketchup, and garlic. Pour over lamb cubes and refrigerate overnight. Thread lamb and mushrooms alternately on metal skewers, with a small space between pieces so they will cook thoroughly. Broil 3 to 4 inches from whitened coals, turning frequently, for about 10 minutes. Scoot lamb and mushrooms to the bottom of the skewer and alternate onion, tomato wedges, and green pepper chunks on the end of the skewers. Return to grill and continue cooking, turning frequently, for 10 minutes. Baste with marinade as they cook.

PACIFIC KABOBS
(SERVES FOUR)

Pineapple and pork are traditional, but these kabobs, made of pineapple and lamb, might well make a new tradition. Kabobs like these went as far as the most western of the Western states—Hawaii.

  2 *pounds lamb from lamb shoulder, cut into 2-inch cubes*
  1 *cup canned pineapple juice*
  2 *tablespoons soy sauce*
  2 *tablespoons lemon juice*
  1 *clove garlic, crushed*
  2 *cups drained, canned pineapple chunks*
  1 *eggplant, cut into 2-inch cubes*
  3 *green peppers, cut into chunks*

Combine pineapple juice, soy sauce, lemon juice, and garlic. Marinate lamb in mixture overnight. Thread lamb on skewers alternately with pineapple chunks, green pepper, and eggplant. Broil 5 minutes, turn, baste with sauce, and continue turning and basting at 5 minute intervals until done—20 to 25 minutes.

BEEF KABOBS
(FOR A SPECIAL DINNER FOR FOUR)

When our friends the Rosenblums visit us, Susie and I get so bored with our husbands' nonstop shop-talk (they're both photographers) that we escape to the kitchen and gossip. We also cook savory things, for Susie is an excellent cook, and once came up with this beef kabob triumph. Ordinarily, it makes me sour to be involved in a social situation where the men congregate in one room and the women gather in another, but with Susie I like it.

For BEEF KABOBS, allow, per person, ¼ pound trimmed and boned sirloin (meat should be cut about 1½-inches thick); 1 medium onion, quartered; 1 medium tomato, halved, or 1 small tomato, whole; and ½ green pepper, halved again. Also have on hand 1 pound fresh whole mushrooms.

Rub skewers with oil and thread with meat, mushrooms, onion, and green pepper, with meat chunks between each vegetable. Top with tomato. Brush with garlic sauce. Hold over coals and turn, brushing with sauce as they cook, 5 minutes for rare, 10 for medium-well, over 10 minutes is burned.

GARLIC SAUCE: Crush 3 cloves garlic and blend well with 1 tablespoon salt. Blend in 2 tablespoons lemon juice, 1 tablespoon soy sauce, and ⅓ cup oil or melted butter.

Serve with corn on the cob and garlic bread.

COOKOUT FISH

I know of two ways to cook fish on an outdoor grill. Both are good. One method is for whole, large fish. The other is for fish cooked in foil packets with potatoes cooking at the same time.

BARBECUE FISH

Montana has miles upon miles of lovely trout streams: Rock Creek, the Madison, the Gallatin, the Smith, the Dearborn, the Yellowstone, Spring Creek, and fabled Big Hole River—which not only has marvelous fly fishing, but is also set in such a splendid landscape that fishing there would be worth the trip even if you never caught anything. All those miles of prime fishing mean that residents have developed good things to do with the catch. This is one of them.

1   *good-sized fish per person, or 1 whopper for several (cleaned
     and gutted)*
     salt
     pepper
     garlic powder
1   *cup melted butter or margarine*

Split fish and remove backbone. Season split sides well with salt, pepper, and garlic powder. When the bed of coals is whitened with ash, place fish cut side down on the grill, about 12 inches from the coals. Baste frequently with melted butter, and leave fish in place for 15 minutes. Turn very carefully and baste generously. Continue to cook, basting frequently, until fish is done—about 10 minutes.

FISH 'N SPUDS 'N FOIL
(SERVES FOUR)

3   *medium potatoes, peeled and sliced ¼-inch thick*
1   *onion, peeled and thinly sliced*
¼   *cup melted butter*
¼   *cup milk*
      Parmesan cheese
1   *large fish, split (cleaned and gutted)*
2   *tablespoons melted butter or margarine*
¼   *teaspoon garlic powder*
      salt, pepper, paprika
⅔   *cup melted butter or margarine*
1   *tablespoon lemon juice*

For the spuds, slice potatoes onto a large piece of heavy foil and top with onion slices. Sprinkle with salt and pepper, and Parmesan cheese. Pour ¼ cup melted butter and the milk over potatoes. Fold foil over potatoes and crimp edges to seal. Put spud package on grill 10 minutes before adding fish. Grill 30 minutes, turn, and grill 20 minutes longer.

Lay split fish, cut side up, on a large piece of heavy foil. Sprinkle with 2 tablespoons melted butter, garlic powder, salt, pepper, and paprika. Turn up edges of foil to hold juices in, and place on the grill about 6 to 8 inches above the coals. Grill 20 minutes, basting occasionally with a mixture of ⅔ cup melted butter and the lemon juice. Turn once, carefully, and grill 20 minutes longer.

PIT-FIRE COOKING

One of the very best cookout methods is pit-fire cooking. It's easy, and the results are tender and delicious.

To cook pit-fire-style, start by digging a pit about 2 feet deep by 2 feet long by 18 inches wide. Build a stout fire in it and keep the fire going until the pit is full of hot, red coals. You'll need at least 6 inches of really hot coals.

PIT-FIRE ROAST

Prepare a 4- to 6-pound chuck, round bone, or rolled beef roast by rubbing it well with salt, pepper, and any other seasonings you like. Wrap it in a triple layer of heavy foil and seal the edges carefully by folding them together as tightly as you can. Push the coals around to make a hole for the roast to nest in. Bank coals all around the roast and cover it with sand or dirt. Go away and fish for 5 hours.

Carefully remove the dirt covering—be careful not to tear the foil package—and just as carefully remove the roast. Use a shovel, as the package will be hot. Take care in removing the foil from the roast—you don't want bits of dirt to fall on the meat, and you don't want to lose the meat juices that will have collected. Slice tender meat that has cooked in its own juice, and spoon the meat juices over it.

BURIED DUTCH OVEN DINNER

When I was a little girl my granddad cooked dinner in a buried dutch oven on a wild Idaho mountain prairie. I still cook out that way, now and then, in the same heavy cast-iron dutch oven he used.

Dig a hole and build a fire in it as you would for a pit-fire roast. When the coals are ready, put the big dutch oven on them and add about ¼ cup cooking oil or bacon fat. Sear a big steak—sirloin, chuck, or round—on both sides. The meat should be cut 2 to 3 inches thick. Sprinkle the seared steak with salt and pepper, then add chunks of peeled potatoes and onions. Add small whole scraped carrots and whole stalks of celery. Put the lid on the dutch oven securely and push and twist until you have nudged the oven halfway down into the coals. Cover the whole arrangement with dirt and go away.

Three hours should cook the dinner, but we have left our buried supper for as long as 8 hours and found on our return that nothing had burned, everything was still warm and juicy and done to perfection. There is something about the steadily declining heat and the meat and vegetables cooking in their own steaming juices that makes them taste marvelously rich and fresh. They will need fewer seasonings—salt and pepper are about all— to bring out their own natural flavors.

We have dropped a few sourdough biscuits on top of the meat and potatoes, and gently lifted the lid to find they had turned into a savory, hand-held blend of biscuit and dumpling.

A little imagination and a few trial and error sessions will produce your own variations of the basic dutch oven dinner. Old-time chuck wagon cooks, who originated buried dutch oven cooking on the Western cattle frontier, often added canned whole tomatoes to their dinners and they very often baked beans dutch oven style. It is a fine camp cooking method because after the initial putting together, dinner cooks with no attention at all from the cook. The coals gradually cool and die, eliminating the possibility of burned food, while the covering of dirt and sand holds the heat long enough to cook the food.

The dutch oven has to be of good size, which makes it heavy because it must also be made of cast iron. The lid is recessed instead of convex so that it fits securely, and coals and dirt can be heaped over it.

A new dutch oven has to be "seasoned," which means it must be heavily oiled with a cup of salt-free shortening or lard and then heated slowly in the oven until it smokes. Let it "cook in" for an hour, then turn off the oven and leave the dutch oven in until it cools. Thereafter, just be careful about cleaning it. No harsh detergents, no scouring powder, and no metal scouring pads! Hot water is as far as you can go. The best way to clean it is with sand and a careful wiping off, but that isn't always practical or possible or even, sometimes, hygenically probable. Just watch that you don't scour it so carefully that you remove the season—for then the iron will rust and the porous metal will absorb bad tastes.

Never pour cold water into a hot dutch oven, either. I did that once, and cracked a treasured dutch oven into two useless pieces. Store it with the lid slightly ajar to keep bad odors from collecting and permeating the slightly oily coating we call the "season." A properly cared-for dutch oven will last forever. We have four: two small ones that are well over fifty years old, including one that is properly called a "spider" because it stands on three tiny cast-iron legs; and two larger ovens that we bought new and seasoned ourselves.

Chapter 12

YOU DON'T HAVE TO SPEND A FORTUNE TO TRAVEL— CAMP MENUS, BACKPACK AND TRAIL FOODS

CAMP COOKING

I have been exposed to a few camp cooks in my life, and I think they may have permanently affected me. My grandfather wasn't a very good camp cook, limited to terrible coffee, hard-fried steaks, leathery eggs, middlin' fair beans, excellent sourdough biscuits, and superlative bacon. He fried bacon correctly—over low heat, turning and draining it constantly so that it fried golden and crisp. Great-uncle Will was a fair camp cook and great-uncle Mark was pretty good at it. I've known a few others along the way— some of them really rank, some of them really excellent. They are all a little cross and demanding and more than a little temperamental. I couldn't understand why until I put my time in as a camp cook for our own guide service.

Camp cooking is hard work. You get up at an unearthly hour—something like 3:30 A.M.—in order to get the camp stove going and the coffee made. Much of my camp cooking has been in high altitudes where water takes an amazingly longer time to boil than it does nearer sea level. Then you cook breakfast for an assortment of grumpy people—and because you cook it on a tiny cooking surface, you have to juggle coffee pot, griddle, and frying pans back and forth and up and down in order to keep everything cooking without boiling over, burning, or cooling to lukewarm. There is no temperature regulation on camp stoves, so you must know which spots on the stove cooking surface are hot, hotter, warm, and cooler. You also must feed sticks of wood to the stove to keep the fire going.

Serving breakfast itself is a trial. The tent is suddenly too small, and you find yourself stepping over legs, swiveling around bodies and boxes and gear, and ducking a sagging ceiling and lines of dangling wet socks. As soon as breakfast is over, it is time to heat water for doing the dishes. Of course, you haul the water in first, and split-and-tote more wood while hot water is happening.

If you are lucky like me, everybody will forage through supplies for his own pocket lunch and cooking for that period of the day will be avoided.

Dinner won't be, however. By starting work on it very early in the afternoon, you can serve it and clean up early enough to fall into bed . . . then crawl out again at 3:30 the next morning. Before you quit for the night, make one last trip to the spring for a bucket of water for the breakfast coffee, and arrange a pile of stove wood so you can fumble a fire going while you're still bleary with sleep. Oh, it's a test of disposition, it is; and I no longer wonder why camp cooks are cross, grumpy, temperamental, and old before their time!

It's kind of fun, too, unless you are cooking for paying guests. I wouldn't advise that for anyone, and someday I'll write a book about my commercial camp cooking days. If you're cooking in camp for yourself and family and friends, the way I do now, it's a fun thing to do. Pre-dawn above 8,000 feet is worth about any cost—the air is so fresh and clean it's like it has never been used before and you feel that all the good things in the whole world belong to you alone.

Now that my experience is qualified, I'll tell you how I go about camp cooking.

Supplies are limited because getting them into camp is hard work. If you travel afoot, you'll be using freeze-dried foods and there is little work in preparing those. If you go with a horse and mule pack string, you will have more to work with, but you will still have to plan every meal down to the last bite as well as every ingredient you will need. You can't make a mistake because there will be no handy corner grocery to run to. Since the cooling arrangement will be primitive, consisting of water and a gunnysack, foods that depend on refrigeration must be forgotten. Horses can carry only so much and there are only so many of them, so you must plan and plan and plan.

On horse or car camp-trips, we always figure on one unknown guest. If four of us are going into camp, we plan on five people. That's partly in case we are unexpectedly delayed coming back out and partly because someone might come down the trail and we will either want to feed him or know that we must.

Camp breakfasts consist of eggs and bacon or ham, or flapjacks. That takes care of that. Lunches are smorgasbord affairs, with cheese, canned fruit, sardines, and dry salami. Dinners are more elaborate, and I depend heavily on one-dish recipes. I make several kinds of bread, turn dried apples into applesauce, use a lot of potatoes and rice, and make sure my coffee is excellent. In fact, let's start with coffee.

CAMP COFFEE

Our coffee pot is a traditional, fire-blackened enamel pot of substantial size. I use it at home, too, and it has traveled in its gunnysack for many, many miles. It has made coffee on stretches of sand battered by the crashing Pacific; on cow-chip and sagebrush fires in Nevada, Idaho, and Montana; on glacial flats and by glimmering lakes in the Canadian Rockies. My coffee pot, unlike my grandfather's, is scrubbed after every use because I like my coffee strong and hot but not bitter, and I think the coffee oils that cling to the inside of the pot make the brew bitter.

I know two ways to make camp coffee. The first way I learned in Nevada. Measure cold water by the cup into the coffee pot. For every 8-oz. cup of water, add 2 level tablespoons (or 1 coffee measure) of regular-grind coffee. Set the pot on the fire and keep an eye on it. When it boils up once, remove it from the fire and set it to one side to stay hot while the grounds settle. Dash in ¼ cup cold water. Let it sit for 5 minutes before serving.

The second method, which I learned a thousand miles further north, takes more time but results in superb coffee. Measure 2 quarts, fresh, cold water into the coffee pot. Bring water to a fast boil. In a bowl mix one 8-oz. cup regular-grind coffee with ¼ cup cold water and 1 beaten egg. Mix until grounds are completely moistened with egg and water. Scrape mixture all at once into furiously boiling water. Stir once, and immediately remove the pot from the fire. Let sit in a warm place 10 minutes to take on character. When you add the coffee-egg mixture, the water will boil up, so be sure the pot is large enough that the coffee doesn't boil over.

CAMP BREADS

After coffee, the next step in establishing stature as a good camp cook is to master several different kinds of camp breads. Sourdough cookery is covered in an entire chapter earlier, and other breads that are good to know about follow.

BANNOCK

BANNOCK was a standby staple that every early-day trapper, trader, and scout lived on while on the trail. Bannock is not really the tastiest of breads and is a bit on the tough side, but when you are out in the bush and real bread is hard to come by Bannock tastes very good indeed.

The basic mix for enough Bannock for two hungry people is:

2   cups all-purpose flour, sifted, measured, then sifted again
2   teaspoon baking powder
½   teaspoon salt
⅓   cup butter or margarine
     water

Combine dry ingredients. Cut margarine into flour mixture until it is like coarse meal. Generously grease a small cast-iron frying pan and put it near the cooking fire to warm. To the basic dry mix add enough cold water to make a firm dough. Work the water in quickly so the dough won't get tough. As soon as it is mixed, shape it into a cake about an inch thick and as big around as the skillet. Lay the Bannock in the heated skillet and put it on the fire until the bottom crusts. Prop the skillet at a steep angle near the fire so direct heat hits the top of the Bannock. When the top has cooked to a tan crust, move the pan back from the fire to prevent fast browning and let it bake about 20 minutes. Thunk it with a finger when you think it is done, and if it sounds hollow you are right.

The proportion of baking powder to flour given in this recipe is effective up to 5,000 feet. Above that, reduce the baking powder to ¾ teaspoon to every cup of flour. If you are scraping the clouds at 10,000 feet, use ½ teaspoon baking powder to every cup of flour.

OLDMAN RIVER BREAD

I made this bread while we were fishing the Oldman River in Alberta, Canada, in the splendor of the Canadian Rockies. We spread it with home-made choke cherry jelly and ate it with freshly caught trout, watched a grizzly bear wade the shallows in the silver dusk, and knew we were incredibly rich.

1	cup cornmeal
1	cup all-purpose flour
2	tablespoons sugar
1	teaspoon salt
2	teaspoons baking powder
2	eggs
4	tablespoons melted margarine or lard
1	cup reconstituted dry milk
1/3	cup hulled sunflower seeds

Combine first 5 ingredients. Beat eggs and blend into the dry ingredients with the melted shortening and reconstituted dry milk. Stir in sunflower seeds. Pour the batter into a well-greased, warmed, cast-iron skillet. Cover skillet and place on that part of the fire or stove that is closest to a low heat. It will take about 30 minutes to cook—you can test it with a toothpick or sliver of wood and call it done when the toothpick comes out clean.

CAMP MIX

We use a flour mixture when we are camping that is packed with all the nourishment that I can get into it. It is used for all flour purposes, and I think it is a valuable addition to our camp tricks. I mix it at home and divide it into large plastic bags, and use it in place of plain flour.

Mix together thoroughly 20 pounds white flour, 10 pounds whole wheat flour, 5 pounds soy flour, and 5 pounds wheat germ.

CAMP SKILLETS

Meals that can be cooked in one skillet are invaluable in camp. To complete any one skillet meal add fruit such as applesauce, a drink, and bread. A good, nourishing, filling dinner is ready with a minimum of activity around the fire.

One of our favorite one-skillet meals is as good for breakfast as it is for supper, and we've enjoyed it when autumn nipped the air far back in the lovely reaches of Cascade Creek, near Banff in Alberta, Canada, and when spring painted the Nevada desert with a pastel brush.

COWBOY SKILLET
(SERVES FOUR)

1   *medium onion, peeled and chopped*
1   *#303 can tomatoes, mashed*
1   *4-oz. can sliced mushrooms, drained*
8   *eggs*
    salt and pepper

Pour 2 tablespoons oil or bacon fat in a skillet. Sauté onions, stirring constantly, until they are golden and soft. Stir in tomatoes and mushrooms and add seasonings. Continue to cook, and stir until tomatoes start to bubble. Break eggs into a bowl and beat with a fork until they are well mixed. Stir into tomato-onion mixture. Cook over low heat, stirring, until mixture sets and gets slightly dry.

RUBICON SPRINGS SKILLET
(SERVES FOUR)

This recipe worked for us while we dried out and rested on the rocks at Rubicon Springs, at the northern end of Desolation Valley high above Lake Tahoe in the Sierra Nevada Range. There was a fine hotel at Rubicon Springs at the turn of the century, and a small parlor organ was freighted in to entertain the guests who patronized the hotel and mineral springs there. How they ever got the organ in there, and how a Concord stagecoach loaded with city-soft guests ever navigated that precipitous road are mysteries to me. The road has long been impassable, and only weathered ruins of the old hotel are left.

 1 *12-oz. can corned beef, diced*
 1 *#303 can whole kernel corn, drained*
 1 *8-oz. can tomato sauce*
 2 *large boiled potatoes, peeled and sliced*
   salt and pepper

Grease a skillet and warm it on the stove or over a low fire. Add corned beef and corn and stir to mix. Arrange slices of potatoes on top. Season with salt and pepper. Pour tomato sauce over potato slices. Cover. Cook over medium heat for 10 minutes. Turn with a spatula as nearly to all at once as possible. Continue cooking 10 minutes.

THREE-MILE SKILLET
(SERVES SIX)

THREE-MILE SKILLET was invented in a sky-high pack-in camp at the head of Three-Mile Canyon on the Idaho-Montana state line. A lovely meadow is there, that one misty morning had fifty-six elk scattered like pepper across it. We watched them until full light sent them quietly back into the timber.

1   *1½-pound round steak*
¼   *cup flour*
¼   *cup cooking oil*
1   *small peeled onion, minced*
     water
2   *cups dry noodles*
1   *package instant cream of mushroom soup, reconstituted*
1   *teaspoon salt*
¼   *teaspoon pepper*

Cut steak into thin strips—about ½-inch wide and 3 inches long. Roll in flour. Put ¼ cup oil or other fat into a good-sized skillet and heat over a medium fire. Brown meat on all sides. Add onion. Push skillet to a "low heat" section of stove or fire and add 2 cups water. Cover and simmer for 1 hour. Add water to bring the liquid with the meat to about 2 cups. Bring to a boil. Sprinkle noodles into liquid and continue cooking until they are tender. Stir in soup and seasonings and simmer 5 minutes.

If you are wondering where I got that round steak, with no store for miles and no refrigeration anywhere, I brought it with me. Here's what to do: Freeze meat before you leave home—wrapped first in plastic film, then in foil. Freeze hard. When you pack for camp, wrap frozen meats thickly and tightly with a layer of newspapers, and tuck in at the last minute. If you keep meat still paper-wrapped in damp gunnysacks in a shady spot in camp, you'll have fresh meat until the fourth day out.

PACK STRING SKILLET
(SERVES FOUR)

A pack string is still exciting to see, even for me, and I've followed so many of them that it should be old hat by now.

When we had our own pack string, half my delight was in going into the Idaho wilderness we loved and half was in the horses and mules I knew so well. Tom, my husband, would lead off, usually on Sabina, who was troublesome because she was so smart. His lead packhorse was always Cocoa, an ex-rodeo bucking horse, who was as stout and strong and faithful as a horse could be, and who always wanted to be first in the string. Pack animals are jealous of their position in line, and will often fuss with each other if their order in the string is changed.

The rest of the horses were strung out after Cocoa in a long line. I rode tail-end-Charlie on whatever horse wasn't needed somewhere else—usually poor, ill-fated Barbie; our son Mark's reliable thoroughbred mare, Targhee; or, finally, my own beautiful Teton. One of the sounds I love to remember is the animals snorting and blowing as they settled into the climb on a frosty fall morning.

Cooking dinner the first day in camp is difficult because there is so much to be done and so little time in which to do it. After the horses are cared for and the camp is arranged and settled, it's dark or near dark and everyone is hungry. This one-skillet dish is comforting during that first-day tumult—it more or less takes care of itself while you get the kitchen set up in one corner of the big tent that is optimistically called the cook tent, but which turns out to be bedroom, kitchen, dining hall, and entertainment center all in one.

¼   *cup cooking oil*
1   *onion, peeled and chopped*
1   *potato, peeled and chopped*
    water
1   *12-oz. can corned beef*
1   *#303 can whole kernel or cream-style corn*
1   *#303 can tomatoes*
1   *teaspoon salt*
½   *teaspoon pepper*
¼   *teaspoon garlic powder*
    grated Parmesan cheese

Heat ¼ cup oil, shortening, or bacon fat in a large skillet. Add onion and potato and about ½ cup water, and cook until vegetables are tender. Add remaining ingredients except Parmesan cheese and stir well. Simmer 30 minutes over the lowest heat obtainable, stirring now and then to keep it from sticking. Sprinkle with the Parmesan cheese. Serve with canned fruit and rolls brought from home for the first night dinner you knew would be frenzied.

WILLOW SPRINGS SKILLET

(SERVES FOUR TO SIX)

There must be a thousand places named Willow Springs in the West. One Willow Springs is in the mountains in central Nevada. There, alone and quiet, we ate fried trout and drank tea in solitude and springtime, and Tom photographed a nest full of baby Red-tailed hawks. The air was heavy with the smell of wild roses, and the rest of the world was so far away that we forgot it. It was a good place to cook things that tasted good without an investment of time.

1   *12-oz. package small elbow macaroni*
    water
1   *onion, peeled and chopped*
1   *#303 can mixed peas and carrots*
⅔   *cup chopped American cheese*
1   *12-oz. can corned beef, chopped*
1   *cup milk*
1   *package dry mushroom soup, reconstituted*
½   *teaspoon salt*
¼   *teaspoon pepper*
    pinch thyme

Cook macaroni and onion in salted water until macaroni is tender. Drain well. Heat a large, greased skillet and combine all ingredients in it. Mix together. Simmer over medium heat and stir frequently so it will not stick. Heat until mixture is bubbly and hot through.

DRIED BEEF GRAVY
(SERVES FOUR)

Military people have insulting names for this old standby dish. Served over instant mashed potatoes or hot buttered noodles, it is quick, filling, and good, and I don't think it deserves its reputation.

    1   5-oz. jar *dried beef*
    ½   *cup butter or margarine*
    2   *tablespoons flour, about*
    2   *cups milk*
    ¼   *teaspoon pepper*

Cut dried beef (sometimes called chip beef) into pieces and fry it in ¼ cup margarine, stirring, until it starts to get crispy. Stir in flour and mix well. Add ¼ cup margarine and stir until margarine is melted. Stir in milk and pepper. Simmer, stirring, until mixture is creamy. If you want a thinner gravy, add more milk.

SOGGY-COOK SKILLET
(SERVES FOUR TO SIX)

This stew isn't soggy. I was, though, the first time that I made it.

Most of our pack trips are enchanted, wonderful things, and ninety-nine out of every hundred I remember with gladness. The one left in every hundred I'd rather not think about until long later, when time gives it an amusing aspect it certainly didn't have when it happened.

One miserable trip started off badly, when Maggie decided she didn't want to be a packhorse and bucked up and down the trail, scattering the contents of her pack all over the Idaho landscape. Forks and food rained down, and a jar of instant orange breakfast drink exploded in midair, making an orange rainbow in the woods. By the time we caught her and picked up and repacked everything, we were late. Nightfall caught us on the trail, still miles from camp. By the time we made an emergency camp, cared for the horses and got a thin fire going, a steady rain was falling. The tent and a comfy camp were still miles up the trail and as far away as morning. We ate dinner hunched in silent misery and then crawled between two pieces of leaky canvas to try to sleep. I should hate this stew, invented then, but time in its wonderful way has made that night hilarious in recollection and I cook the stew now with laughter.

6 cups water
3 potatoes, scrubbed but not peeled, cut into chunks
4 carrots, scrubbed but not scraped, cut into chunks
4 stalks celery, cut into chunks
1 onion, peeled, cut into chunks
1 12-oz. can corned beef, cubed
1 package mushroom or onion soup mix, reconstituted
   salt and pepper

Combine water and vegetables in a large skillet and simmer until tender—about 45 minutes. Stir in remaining ingredients and season. Simmer about 10 minutes.

CHICKEN SKILLET
(SERVES SIX)

Serve this chicken recipe over instant mashed potatoes, rice, or hot buttered noodles. Open a can of bright vegetables and serve fruit for dessert.

1 whole canned chicken
2 tablespoons flour or cornstarch, for thickening
   salt and pepper

Heat the chicken in a large skillet, stirring constantly and removing bones as it heats so the final result is boneless chicken pieces. Let simmer 5 minutes. Thicken with flour or cornstarch, and season to taste with salt and pepper.

MEATLESS CAMPS

Meatless dishes are good to know in camp when the fresh meat supply is depleted and you're tired of canned meats. We sometimes like creamed eggs. Since eggs are so easy to take into camp—and keep fresh so long—you should pack lots of them. They travel well in their own nested egg cartons. We have transported hundreds of eggs over rough trails via pack string, and the only eggs we ever broke were those I accidentally sat on.

CREAMED EGGS
(SERVES FOUR)

8   *hard-cooked eggs*
3   *cups medium white sauce*
1   *teaspoon salt*
½   *teaspoon pepper*
¼   *teaspoon paprika*
¼   *teaspoon curry powder*

Prepare medium white sauce and stir in seasonings. Gently peel hard-cooked eggs, trying to keep them whole. Add to white sauce. Let them simmer a few minutes, then serve over hot buttered rice.

RICE

We always take rice into camp. It takes up less space than potatoes, we don't worry about having it freeze to the marble stage, and it's easy to work with. All those reasons justify the 3-pound sack of old-fashioned brown rice that I tuck in with the spuds.

To cook it in camp, bring 4 cups of water and 1 teaspoon salt to a boil. Pour in 1½ cups rice, cover, and put the rice on the part of the stove or fire that will keep it at a low simmer. Check—quickly, so all the steam won't escape—now and then. When the water is gone, the rice should be done—still chewy, but soft.

For breakfast or as a dinner dessert, add a handful of raisins while the rice is cooking. When done, stir in honey to taste and sprinkle with cinnamon.

CAMP FRIED RICE
(SERVES FOUR)

Heat ¼ cup oil or bacon fat in a large skillet. Chop 1 peeled onion and a stalk of celery and cook gently in the hot fat, stirring constantly so it will get tender without browning. Add about 2 cups cooked rice, and season with 2 tablespoons soy sauce. Cook and stir for 5 minutes. Break 1 egg into a cup and beat slightly. Stir it into the rice. Continue cooking until egg is done.

SKILLET RICE DINNER
(SERVES FOUR)

6	*slices bacon*
1	*large onion, peeled and chopped*
3	*cups hot water*
1	*cup rice*
1	*cup canned tomatoes*
½	*cup diced cheddar cheese*
1	*teaspoon salt*
1	*tablespoon sugar*
¼	*teaspoon pepper*
¼	*teaspoon garlic powder*
	pinch sage

Fry bacon in large skillet. When golden, remove and break into pieces. Add onion to same skillet and sauté until golden and soft. Add water and rice. Cover and simmer until rice is soft. Stir in remaining ingredients and stir well. Simmer for 5 minutes.

BACKWOODS PILAF

(SERVES FOUR)

¼ cup bacon drippings or cooking oil
1 onion, peeled and finely chopped
1 cup rice
1 teaspoon salt
¼ teaspoon pepper
1 10 ¾-oz. can bouillon, can refilled once with water
⅓ cup raisins
⅓ cup hulled sunflower seeds

Cook onion and rice in hot fat in skillet, stirring, until rice is golden. Add seasonings, soup, and water. Cover and simmer 30 minutes. Add raisins and continue simmering until rice is done—20 to 30 minutes—adding hot water if necessary. Add sunflower seeds and simmer 5 minutes more.

CAMP DUTCH OVEN

Beans are always good in camp, and so is stew. A real benefit is dutch oven cooking, which we discussed in the preceding chapter. After you get a dutch oven established in its bed of coals, covered snugly with dirt or sand, you can forget about stirring, peeking, adding or tending—or even feeding the stove—for hours. And, in the hills, hours of freedom to spend as you like are what you are there for.

DUTCH OVEN STEW

(SERVES FOUR)

2   *pounds stew meat, cut into 1-inch cubes*
2   *tablespoons flour*
2   *large potatoes, scrubbed but not peeled, cut into chunks*
1   *large onion, peeled and cut into chunks*
2   *or 3 carrots, scrubbed but not peeled, cut into large slices*
2   *stalks celery, cut into thick pieces*
1   *#303 can tomatoes, mashed*
    salt, pepper
1   *cup water*

To make a stew dutch oven style, dig the hole and build the pit-fire as in the preceding chapter. Generously grease the dutch oven and heat it. Drop in meat and sprinkle with salt, pepper, and flour. Cook, stirring, until meat is browned. Add vegetables and water; pour tomatoes over top. Season with salt and pepper. Put the lid on securely and bury dutch oven in hot coals. Put coals on the lid, rake dirt over the whole pit, and go away. Dig it up any time after 2 hours. A pan of BANNOCK goes nicely with the stew.

DUTCH OVEN BISCUITS

Dig and fire the dutch oven hole. Generously grease the dutch oven and let it warm. Mix biscuit dough from your own favorite recipe, prepared mix, or sourdough. Put biscuits in dutch oven, sides just touching. Replace lid. Make a hole in the hot coals and shovel about an inch of dirt over the coals. Put dutch oven in hole. Put a few hot coals on the lid. Fifteen minutes should be enough to cook the biscuits. Be careful because if you have too many coals on the lid, you'll burn the biscuits.

DUTCH OVEN BREAD

Prepare fire and dutch oven as for biscuits. Place a round loaf of sourdough in the greased dutch oven. Place lid on securely. Shovel out half the hot coals and sprinkle remaining coals with 1 inch of dirt. Put dutch oven in hole and scrunch it around until it is level. Cover dutch oven with coals and then shovel dirt over the entire arrangement. The bread will be done in an hour.

CAMP DESSERTS

Desserts in camp are infrequent. When they do happen they are simple, and you'll rave about desserts that you would not give a second glance to at home. I depend on dried fruit because it is light in weight, reasonable in bulk, highly nutritious, and adaptable. Of all the dried fruits, I like dried apples best.

E-Z APPLE DESSERT

Bring a cup of sliced dried apples to a simmer in enough water to cover. Remove from heat and let cool. Season with brown sugar and cinnamon to taste.

Bake a pan of BANNOCK. As soon as the bottom crust has browned, turn the Bannock over in the pan and cover browned side with apples. Continue to cook for 10 minutes. Lay thin slices of cheddar cheese on top and let the Bannock continue to cook for another 5 to 10 minutes—until Bannock is cooked through and the cheese has melted into the apples.

SKILLET APPLE PUDDING
(SERVES FOUR TO SIX)

2	cups water
2	cups dried apple slices
½	teaspoon nutmeg
½	teaspoon cinnamon
½	cup brown sugar or honey
½	cup grated cheddar cheese
½	cup brown sugar
½	cup flour
⅓	cup butter or margarine

Bring water to boil in saucepan and add apple slices. Cover, remove from heat, and let stand 1 hour. Grease a skillet and spoon in apples and juices. Sprinkle with seasonings and sugar or honey. Sprinkle grated cheese over top. Put over a low heat part of the stove or fire and cook gently for 10 minutes. Mix ½ cup brown sugar with flour and margarine until it is crumbled. Sprinkle evenly over top of apples. Cook gently 5 minutes.

APPLESAUCE
(SERVES FOUR)

Camp applesauce is used constantly, at every meal and with all recipe combinations. It's an excellent food stretcher, nutritious and little trouble to prepare; and for some reason, camp applesauce is better than anything you buy or make at home.

4	cups water
½	teaspoon salt
2	cups dried apples
1	teaspoon vanilla
½	teaspoon nutmeg
1	teaspoon cinnamon
	brown sugar

Bring water and salt to a simmer. Add apples and simmer 30 minutes or until apples are tender. Stir in flavorings and add brown sugar to taste. Simmer 5 minutes longer.

CELEBRATION! DESSERT

(SERVES FOUR TO SIX)

If wild berries or strawberries are fruiting near your mountain camp, pick 4 cups of them. Otherwise, use an equivalent amount of reconstituted dried apples, apricots, or peaches.

    4   cups fruit
          water to cover
    1½   cups sugar or honey
    4   tablespoons cornstarch
    1   teaspoon cinnamon
    ⅓   cup sugar
    3   tablespoons butter or margarine
    ½   cup milk
    1½   cups sifted flour
    1½   teaspoons baking powder
          pinch of salt

Add cold water to barely cover fruit. Add 1½ cups sugar or honey, cornstarch, and cinnamon. Bring to a boil. Reduce to a simmer by moving the pot to a cooler part of stove or fire. Stir mixture until it has thickened slightly. Let it continue to simmer while you cream ⅓ cup sugar with butter or margarine. Blend in milk. Mix flour with baking powder and salt, and stir dry mixture and milk mixture together. Drop by large spoonsful over the simmering fruit. Cover and continue simmering gently about 10 minutes. Serve warm.

COMMENTS ON CAMP COOKING

Autumn in camp at high altitudes means frigid nights, and you can catch a hard freeze at any time. If canned goods freeze they can be touchy or downright dangerous, so watch for cans with bulging ends that mean damaged contents. Eggs that have frozen will be rubbery, but they won't hurt you. Cheese will be rubbery and stringy after freezing, but it isn't dangerous either and may be eaten safely. Potatoes that freeze are hard as rocks, and they will spoil rapidly if you let them thaw again. Keep them frozen until you need them, then scrape the skins off in hot water. Drop them, whole, into rapidly boiling water—one at a time, so the water doesn't cool and stop boiling. The freezing emphasizes their sugar content, so the flavor will be intriguingly different.

Margarine keeps better than butter. An assortment of canned herbs and spices are worth their small weight.

Pack trips and high camps go on, I hope forever, but our Idaho pack string days are past now and only Mark's gentle old Targhee is left of all the horses.

The others are no longer with us, and I remember them with a small ache because I loved them. Bright, naughty Sabina; honest Cocoa; the mules—Jim and John and businesslike Molly and dear little Jackpot with his bag of innocent tricks; funny Thunder and dumb blonde Lightening; dour old Maud; Hitch and Little Red and Keno; spooky Bloomers, afraid of her shadow; maddening Maggie and mean Brandy; poor Barbie; Nutmeg and dainty Cricket, 50 Dollars, and Emmy Lou; kindly Ned, reliable Babe, polite Tahoe. Beautiful, haughty Teton was mine.

The last time Tom took the string into Idaho wilderness, he left me behind at the trail-head, straining on tiptoe to see even after they were out of sight, hurting because something dear was ending and would never come again.

Sometimes now in quiet moments I remember, and hear Sabina's companionable snort-snore drift back through all the autumns, and foolishly I whisper, "Wait for me—wait for me."

TRAIL FOODS

There is a joyous freedom in backpacking that you will never understand unless you try it.

Before I first found freedom in wilderness foot travel, I thought back-packers knew some special secret I didn't know. I believed in my heart of hearts that people who hiked mountain trails belonged to an exclusive cult, knew secret ways of walking, and had learned mysterious methods of using their bodies so that they never felt fatigue or strain. The idea of going wilderness routes frightened me because I felt inadequate. I had a feeling that if only someone would whisper the magic formula in my ear, I, too, would be able to go into the wild places.

The day I found my wilderness freedom was one of the most important days of my life, for on that day began some of my happiest adventures. The "secret" of trail travel is this: All you have to do is go.

I still go through a period of leaden legs, straining lungs, and pounding heart—despising myself for getting soft and flabby and swearing that I will, indeed, stop smoking. I know now, though, that just about everyone starts every backpack season with those same feelings—and that it is only a matter of miles before my legs work the way they were designed to work, my lungs will get blown out and tuned up and will provide the oxygen I need after all, and that my heart is basically O.K. and not at all precarious.

Backpacking becomes worth the effort, the work, the sore muscles, and the sweat the first time you walk along some jagged ridge trail and feel an intoxicating freedom and peculiar sense of oneness. The tiredness goes away.

Really good backpacking equipment is worth its moderate investment. It will last many, many miles, and you'll develop a fond friendship with it. Get a good pack frame, fitted to your height, body structure, and the average load you will carry. Depend on tried-and-true brand names—they have earned their reputations. Talk to experienced backpackers, and observe the brands of equipment they respect and trust. Think over the types of backpack bags that go on the pack frame, and mentally assess how each type fits what you want from a pack bag. *Get good quality.* Cheap fabrics and cut-rate workmanship result in backpacks that are either uncomfortable or downright painful, require constant pampering and repairing, and fall apart in a distressingly short time.

My backpack is very light in comparison to my husband's. He carries camera, camera gear, tripods, and film as well as camping supplies, and his backpack is often a staggering eighty pounds—nearly half his body weight and definitely not recommended for anybody. Mark, our older boy, is 6′ 4″ and weighs 170 pounds; he carries a more realistic fifty-five pounds. Your maximum should be no more than one-third your body weight. Tommy Lee, most often called T-Lee, carries a rucksack with his lunch, a small canteen of water, and his jacket. I carry forty pounds at most.

Each of us carries his own sleeping bag, and Mark also totes T-Lee's. (He will be stout enough this year, at age seven, to carry his own 3½-pound down bag.) One of us gets the backpack tent. My husband, Tom, carries the first aid supplies and his own cache of emergency trail foods because he is often on the trail by himself. Each of us carries materials for starting a fire; a flashlight; nylon cord that is really tough; a squashed roll of toilet paper (it takes up less space if it is squashed out of round); a garden trowel (for burying human wastes); a good knife and a small whetstone; our own eating utensils; our own extra clothing—pared to a minimum; a sheet of thin plastic roughly 4 feet by 8 feet (this is an item of many uses and folds up small enough to go into a backpack side pocket); a map of the country we're in; band-aids for blisters; and the few personal items we individually consider indispensible. (Mark carries his luxuriously lightweight fishing gear and his camera. I carry note pads.) Tom and Mark have small, excellently made hand axes. Somehow, sufficient soap and towels and toothbrushes are wedged in.

We divide the cooking utensils (lightweight but well-made aluminum) and food supplies between us. In some areas, where open fires are either forbidden or imprudent, a tidy backpack stove goes along. Each of us carries in his pockets sufficient trail food for the day—that's our lunch.

The subject of food is serious, and it is determined as much by weight as by nutritional value. For the most part, freeze-dried foods are the only satisfactory solution—but be careful! Try different brands at home before you invest in supplies for a trip afield. Unfortunately, brands vary considerably in taste appeal and some are plain nasty, resembling nothing so much as sawdust.

All brands are somewhat expensive. You can save money and have a better product by making some of your own foods and packaging them yourself in plastic bags. For instance, a breakfast cereal you make yourself and package in one-serving plastic pouches is nutritionally superior to anything on the market and costs a fraction of the commercially prepared products.

Dinners are a different story, and it's difficult to produce them on your own. There are flavorful freeze-dried products that pack with so little weight that a small packet will provide sufficient food for four people for dinner with only the addition of hot water. Shop around until you find a brand you like. I don't endorse any brand, but the one we use is really very good and is roughly one-third the price of several brands that have greater snob appeal.

TRAIL BREAKFAST

Our trail breakfasts are usually a granola-type cereal packed in one-person servings in plastic bags. All that is required to make breakfast is to add hot water and stir, and a breakfast is ready to eat—filling, high in nutritional value, inexpensive, and delicious.

4	*cups instant or quick-cook oatmeal*
2	*cups wheat germ*
1	*cup shredded coconut*
1	*cup hulled sunflower seeds*
1	*cup sesame seeds*
1	*cup peanuts or cashews, chopped*
1/3	*cup brown sugar*
1	*tablespoon salt*
1/2	*cup honey*
1/2	*cup vegetable or safflower oil*
1	*cup raisins*
1/3	*cup sugar*
1¾	*cups instant nonfat dry milk*

In a very large bowl combine first 8 ingredients.

With an egg beater whip together honey and vegetable or safflower oil. Stir into the dry mixture. You will have to use your hands, in order to get it mixed together well.

Spread mixture on a big, shallow, lightly oiled pan, such as a cookie sheet with edges. Bake for 45 minutes in a 200° F. oven, stirring gently now and then. Cool. Stir in raisins.

Put ½ to 1 cup of the mixture into small plastic bags, depending on individual appetites. In each bag add 1 teaspoon sugar and a heaping tablespoon instant nonfat dry milk. Seal with tape or a hot iron, depending on the type of plastic bag you use.

To serve, bring water to a boil. Pour the mixture from the plastic bag into a cup or bowl. Stir in hot water to the consistency you like. You can also eat the cereal dry, right out of the plastic bag. When finished, put the plastic bag back in your pocket. If you carried it in full, you can carry it out empty.

On long trips we sometimes vary our breakfasts with freeze-dried scrambled eggs, but we find the eggs lack the staying power of our home-made cereal breakfasts.

TRAIL LUNCHES

Lunches on the trail are delightfully uncomplicated. We make them up at home before the trip, and each morning we put our trail lunch in our pockets—with extras for snacks. We do not stop to cook an elaborate lunch, and find our trail lunches will carry us through the day in fine shape.

There are several good trail lunch foods: special cookies we call FREIGHTERS because they carry so much food value; a type of space stick; a good pemmican that is worth the time it takes to make; a marvelous thing variously called Glop, Gork, Gorp, or Gunk; COFFEE PICKUPS; cheese and salami cubes; sandwiches made of peanut butter and meat on hard rolls; and apples.

FREIGHTERS

I like to have FREIGHTERS on hand at home, too. They are so "good for you" that I don't mind if T-Lee eats too many of them; and when Mark comes home from campus, it is good to have a lot of things around to snack on. Sometimes he brings his friend, Will, with him—who is our friend, too, dear to us and beautiful inside and out the way most young people are. They eat staggering amounts of food, and Freighters help. This cookie is less sweet than most, and people who are used to overly sugared treats take a few Freighters before they really like them.

½   cup vegetable or safflower oil
⅔   cup honey
2   eggs, beaten
¼   cup milk
1   cup nonfat dried milk powder or 1 envelope of the quantity
     needed to make 1 quart milk
1   teaspoon vanilla
¼   teaspoon salt
1½ cups quick-cook oatmeal
¾   cup whole wheat flour
¼   cup wheat germ
1   cup hulled sunflower seeds
¾   cup coconut shreds
½   cup chopped peanuts, walnuts, cashews, or pecans
¾   cup raisins (optional)

Combine all ingredients and mix well. Drop by teaspoonsful on a lightly oiled cookie sheet. Bake at 350° F. for 8 to 10 minutes.

A handful of Freighters provides a large portion of your nutritional requirements for an entire day. Play around with the recipe and add ingredients you like—such as a handful of chopped dates or chopped, dried pineapple, a teaspoon of cinnamon, or ½ teaspoon each cinnamon and cloves, or ½ cup sesame seeds.

SPACE STICKS
(MAKES THREE DOZEN)

1   cup chunk-style peanut butter
1   cup honey
2   cups nonfat dry milk powder
½   cup raisins
½   cup grated scraped carrot
1   cup uncooked oatmeal
¼   cup wheat germ
2   cups shredded coconut, approximately

Mix all ingredients, stirring until ingredients are very well blended. Using your fingers shape mixture into small sticks about the size of your little finger. Roll sticks in shredded coconut. Wrap individually in plastic wrap.

PEMMICAN
(MAKES 24 CAKES)

Pemmican comes down through centuries to today, for what we call pemmican is a variation of an American Indian food. It is time-consuming to make, but one batch makes a good quantity and it is such versatile stuff that it is really worth the time. A cake of pemmican is delicious nibbled on the trail, and it is good to melt one into stew or into a cup or two of bouillon for a drink that is packed with food value.

4   *cups powdered meat*
1½   *cups beef suet*
1   *cup currant jelly*
¾   *cup bouillon*
½   *cup brown sugar*
¼   *cup ground raisins*
½   *teaspoon each allspice, garlic powder, savory, and black pepper*
1   *teaspoon dried minced chives*

To make the powdered meat, cut long strips of lean beef as thin as you can. Lay the strips flat on the rack in a very slow oven and leave them until they are dried. (The oven heat must be very low so the strips dry instead of cook.) When they are dried, like jerky, put them through a meat grinder using the finest blade to make a coarse powder.

Melt suet over very low heat. Add currant jelly. Blend powdered meat with remaining ingredients. Add the seasoned meat mixture gradually to the melted suet, stirring constantly. Cover tightly and bake in a preheated 300° F. oven for 1½ to 2 hours. Remove from oven and ladle immediately into muffin tins, filling no more than 1 inch full. When they have cooled completely, remove and wrap the round pemmican cakes in foil. Store in your freezer.

GLOP
(MAKES 20 SERVINGS)

Some people call this Glop, some call it Gorp or Gork, and I've even heard it called Gunk. It's a good thing to know about. It's one of those quick-energy things you carry in your pocket so you can fill the hollow pit of your stomach for enough energy to carry you merrily along the trail until dinner time. As Mark says, it's good when you have run out of calories. Put a handful in small plastic bags before you leave home, and take several bags for each person—one bag per person for each day you will be out.

    4 *1-pound packages coated, nonmelt chocolate candies (Be sure they
       are the nonmelt, coated variety—anything else melts into a
       disaster.)*
    4 *cups raisins—I use 2 cups light raisins and 2 cups dark*
    5 *cups peanuts or chopped cashews*
    3 *cups shredded coconut*
    2 *cups chopped dried fruit—pineapple is excellent*
    2 *cups hulled sunflower seeds*

Combine ingredients and mix well in a large bowl, and put one cup each into plastic sandwich bags. What you don't use stores in the freezer, ready to go the next time you take to the trail.

COFFEE PICKUPS

For a quick, delicious pick-me-up, mix 1 teaspoon powdered instant coffee with 1 teaspoon powdered sugar. Add the tiniest pinch ground cinnamon you can pinch. Roll into tiny bits of foil and twist up for carrying. One of these dissolved in your mouth invigorates your waning enthusiasm. I like instant Turkish coffee for mine.

CHEESE AND SALAMI CUBES

Cheese and salami cubes are just what they say they are. Crouton-sized squares of a slow-to-melt cheddar cheese mixed with an equal number of the same size cubes of Italian dry salami. Put a handful of the mixed cubes in a plastic sandwich bag to carry in your shirt pocket.

RUSSIAN TEA

When we are on the trail lunch is often a solitary, traveling affair—eaten from pockets as we walk along a gentle stretch feeling vibrantly alive. Sometimes we stop and lunch together, leaning against sun-warmed boulders, sprawling in pungent-smelling pine needles, or sitting on a stream bank with our feet in tingling water. Now and again we think a cup of bouillon or hot tea would be super, so we stop and make a tiny fire just big enough and hot enough to heat water for our premixed RUSSIAN TEA. If you do not already know how to make Russian Tea, try our version. (If you prefer bouillon, make it from a cube or two that you have handy in your shirt pocket.)

2	*cups orange flavored breakfast drink*
1½	*cups plain (not lemon-flavored) instant tea*
1½	*cups sugar*
1	*3-oz. package lemonade mix*
1½	*teaspoons ground cinnamon*
½	*teaspoon ground cloves*

Combine and mix ingredients very well.

Store in a tightly closed container, such as a big glass jar. To serve, measure 2 to 3 teaspoons mix into a cup and fill with boiling water. On the trail, take premeasured portions along in bits of twisted foil to stir into a cup of boiling water. Be careful that you don't drop that bit of foil by mistake into the lovely outdoor world.

We save money on trail trips by taking our homemade breakfasts and lunches, and investing in freeze-dried dinners. We also take individually packaged instant soups and relax over a cup of soup before dinner—that takes the urgent edge off our appetites, helps fill us, and is a nice way to enjoy the end of day. We then have a freeze-dried main dish and perhaps a dessert—and all that is needed to make them ready-to-eat is the addition of the appropriate quantity of boiling water. We drink tea—made with instant milk and sugar for T-Lee—and sleep under stars that seem close enough to touch. There are the smells and sounds of wildness around us as we sleep and the security of the good earth beneath our bodies, and we know that we are alive in our bones and sinews and pores. The last limiting fetters of crowded attitudes drop away and our perspectives widen and then, sooner or later somewhere along the trail, so invariably that we have learned to count on it, there comes again the certain knowledge that it is beautiful to be human.

Chapter 13

P. S.

People all too often made a rigid, serious, do-or-die thing out of cooking. It needn't be. Family cooking should be happy. Cook with love, with an emphasis on hospitality, and relax.

If a recipe calls for an 8-ounce jar of something and you have only a 4-ounce jar, the dish will probably taste just as fine with 4 ounces as with 8. Frontier cooking was adaptable and got along fine with substitutions. Some substitutions are almost formalized: Substitute ¼ teaspoon baking soda and ½ teaspoon cream or tartar for 1 teaspoon baking powder; ⅞ cup cooking oil will replace 1 cup of butter, as will ⅘ cup clarified bacon fat if you increase the recipe's liquids by ¼ cup; 2⅔ tablespoons cocoa and ½ table-spoon shortening will substitute for 1 square sweet or semi-sweet chocolate; 2 tablespoons flour will replace 1 tablespoon cornstarch for thickening; 1 cup honey is as good as 1 cup molasses; 1 cup of milk can be replaced by ½ cup evaporated milk plus ½ cup water, or by 4 tablespoons powdered milk and 1 cup water; ¾ cup molasses and ¼ teaspoon baking soda will replace 1 cup of sugar if you reduce liquids by ¼ cup, and so will 1 cup of honey or maple syrup plus ¼ teaspoon baking soda. Perhaps it would be good to have written down somewhere handy the note that there are 3 teaspoons in 1 tablespoon, 2 cups in a pint, and 4 cups in a quart.

In pioneer days, cooks had to make do with what they had. Food turned out to be filling and nutritious, and people enjoyed eating around a table that was set with friendship and laughter as well as with knives, forks, and spoons. It really doesn't matter if your plates are chipped or if the silver doesn't match. What does matter is pushing out your heart's horizons so there is room for gladness.

Days are often overcrowded with pressures, tensions, troubles, and anxieties. It is more important now than ever to make an island of your dinner table—to reach out and touch the people around you and to re-member what love feels like, to take comfort and give it in the human relationships that are, after all, what life is all about.

Rent, taxes, illness, wars, worries, grief, loneliness—all are undeniably a part of life. So, just as undeniably, are gladness, friendship, tenderness, laughter, silly moments and those that are soft. The most important thing of all is now, with you. Celebrate, by breaking bread, together, on this bit of earth.

INDEX

Checklist and Index for Evaluation

(Suggestions for using this chart appear on Page 446.)

ANALYSIS OF AUDIENCE = AN./

1. Audience accurately identified (80-86)
2. Audience analysis thorough (86-94)
3. Audience's presumed interests, beliefs, attitudes, and values carefully considered (86-89)
4. Audience's attitude toward speaker and subject correctly analyzed (90-91)
5. Audience's motives ascertained (86-91)
6. Occasion correctly analyzed (50; 73-74; 93-94)

SPEECH SUBJECT AND PURPOSE = SUBJ./

7. Subject appropriate to audience and occasion (49-50)
8. Subject appropriately narrowed (48)
9. General speech purpose appropriate (48)
10. Specific purposes clear and attainable (48-49)

CONTENT OF SPEECH = CONT./

11. Major ideas adequately supported or explained by good use of:
    A. Explanation (119-120)
    B. Analogy/comparison (121-122)
    C. Illustration (122-124)
    D. Specific instances (124-125)
    E. Statistics (125-127)
    F. Restatement (129-130)
    G. Visual supports/aids (271-272)
12. Range of sources of information utilized (130-134)
    A. Interviews (130-131)
    B. Letters and questionnaire (130-131)
    C. Printed materials (132-134)
    D. Radio and TV broadcasts (134)

ORGANIZATION OF SPEECH = ORG./

13. Major ideas properly established (197-199)
14. Speech plan clear (169)
15. Full and balanced coverage of subject (169)
16. Moves toward satisfying termination (170)
17. Major ideas systematically arranged (169-175)
18. Organization adapted to specific purpose (68-69)
19. Organization adapted to specific occasion (170)

DEVELOPMENT OF SPEECH = DEV./

20. Beginning (attention step) satisfactory
    A. Captures attention (152-156; 180)
    B. Well-suited to subject/purpose of speech (180-181)
    C. Satisfies demands of audience and occasion (180-181)
    D. Creates good will (181)
21. Need step satisfactory
    A. Clearly developed (156)
    B. Strongly related to audience (156)
22. Satisfaction step well developed
    A. In a speech to inform (156)
    B. In a speech to persuade (157; 316-318)
    C. In parallel with need step (157)
    D. To ensure clarity of proposal (157)
    E. To show proposal as practical (157; 307)
23. Visualization step well handled
    A. Projects audience into future (159)
    B. Conveys reality and vividness (159)
    C. When positive method is used (159)
    D. When negative method is used (159)
    E. When contrast method is used (160)